AN INTRODUCTION TO

TO

HELPING SKILLS

SAGE was founded in 1965 by Sara Miller McCune to support the dissemination of usable knowledge by publishing innovative and high-quality research and teaching content. Today, we publish over 900 journals, including those of more than 400 learned societies, more than 800 new books per year, and a growing range of library products including archives, data, case studies, reports, and video. SAGE remains majority-owned by our founder, and after Sara's lifetime will become owned by a charitable trust that secures our continued independence.

Los Angeles | London | New Delhi | Singapore | Washington DC | Melbourne

AN
INTRODUCTION
TO
HELPING
SKILLS

COUNSELLING, COACHING AND MENTORING

JANE WESTERGAARD

Los Angeles | London | New Delhi
Singapore | Washington DC | Melbourne

SAGE

Los Angeles | London | New Delhi
Singapore | Washington DC | Melbourne

SAGE Publications Ltd
1 Oliver's Yard
55 City Road
London EC1Y 1SP

SAGE Publications Inc.
2455 Teller Road
Thousand Oaks, California 91320

SAGE Publications India Pvt Ltd
B 1/I 1 Mohan Cooperative Industrial Area
Mathura Road
New Delhi 110 044

SAGE Publications Asia-Pacific Pte Ltd
3 Church Street
#10-04 Samsung Hub
Singapore 049483

Editor: Susannah Trefgarne
Editorial assistant: Edward Coats
Production editor: Rachel Burrows
Marketing manager: Camille Richmond
Cover design: Lisa Harper-Wells
Typeset by: C&M Digitals (P) Ltd, Chennai, India
Printed and bound by CPI Group (UK) Ltd,
Croydon, CR0 4YY

Library of Congress Control Number: 2016937684

British Library Cataloguing in Publication data

A catalogue record for this book is available from
the British Library

ISBN 978-1-4739-2510-6
ISBN 978-1-4739-2511-3 (pbk)

At SAGE we take sustainability seriously. Most of our products are printed in the UK using FSC papers
and boards. When we print overseas we ensure sustainable papers are used as measured by the PREPS
grading system. We undertake an annual audit to monitor our sustainability.

CONTENTS

ABOUT THE AUTHOR

Jane Westergaard is an associate senior lecturer at Canterbury Christ Church University. She teaches on programmes for students who plan to engage in employment in a range of helping professions including counsellors, mentors and coaches in education, health and social care settings. Jane developed and teaches on the BA (Hons) Counselling, Coaching and Mentoring, the Certificate in Supervision Studies, and the Advanced Certificate in Supervision Studies programmes.

Jane is a qualified and practising UKRC-registered counsellor, working with young people and adult clients. This includes the setting-up of a counselling service for teachers in an Inner London secondary school. She also has experience of supervision spanning 20 years and has researched and published a range of academic papers on the topic. Currently Jane supervises head teachers, senior leaders, teachers, learning mentors, child protection teams, and others in a range of school settings across London and the south-east. She has spoken on the subject of counselling, coaching, mentoring and supervision at a number of national and international conferences. Jane's current research focuses on exploring integrative approaches to counselling with young people, and she has written widely on this subject and published a range of texts focusing on counselling and supervision.

ACKNOWLEDGEMENTS

A number of people have been key to the development and production of this text. First, I would like to thank my colleagues Alison Fielding and Barbara Bassot. Alison helped in early discussions to form the structure of the book, whilst Barbara authored Chapter 6 on her academic specialism, reflective practice. Thanks to you both.

Second, the content of this book would not offer the breadth, depth and practical-application element without Part II. I would like to thank the ten practitioners who gave up their time to provide such rich and detailed case studies – all examples from their own professional contexts. Thank you to:

- Georgia Bentley – NHS community drug worker
- Rebecca Corfield Tee – life-coach
- Amy Cotgrove – learning support assistant
- Sarah Hayesmore – care manager assistant in social services
- James Hickman – teacher in a children's hospital
- Sally Hickman – trainee probation officer
- Cindy Johnson – surgical nurse specialist
- Deb Lee – telephone helpline counsellor
- Carolyn Mumby – counsellor and coach therapist
- Kim Walder – registered manager of a children's home

Third, a debt of gratitude to my 'critical friend' Ruth Higgins, who has supported the writing process throughout and made valuable suggestions, all from an empathic, congruent and non-judgemental perspective, in keeping with the subject matter. Thank you Ruth.

Finally, I would like to thank the team at Sage who have given me their wholehearted professional support from development to final production. Many thanks to you all.

INTRODUCTION TO THE BOOK
DEFINING THE HELPING RELATIONSHIP

Introduction objectives: Readers will have the opportunity to ...

- explore the rationale for the book and identify its key features;
- consider how they might use the book;
- define the term 'helping relationship' in the professional context;
- examine the purpose of the 'helping relationship';
- explore the key characteristics of a 'helping relationship';
- identify core attributes for the effective helper.

This book offers an introduction to developing effective professional 'helping' relationships. There has been an increase in the numbers of professional helping roles in a range of contexts, including health, education, social care and private organisations. Those who work in these roles, as counsellors, coaches, mentors and others, must develop knowledge and skills in key areas to ensure that they are able to support clients effectively. This text seeks to support, educate and illustrate important skills and concepts that should be developed and understood by those whose role is to engage with and help others. So, anyone who is training to become a counsellor, coach or mentor, anyone who is already in practice in a 'helping' context, or anyone who is considering going into this kind of work... this book has been written with you in mind.

The introduction to this book serves a dual purpose. First, it explains how the text has been structured and how it might be used, and then it outlines key features that include activities with which the reader can engage. It introduces the reader to the contents in Part I and Part II and suggests how both parts of the book complement each other; in Part II, the real-life case studies supplied by practitioners in a range of helping professions can be used to illustrate and illuminate key ideas discussed in chapters in Part I. Second, it engages with a debate about what being a helper actually means. It offers insights and invites the reader to engage with activities to enhance understanding. This aspect of the introduction serves to demonstrate in practical terms how the rest of the book might be used.

Part I

Part I of the text focuses on the skills, knowledge and understanding of theoretical concepts and ideas that are central to helping practice. Chapter 1 sets out to define key terms relating to helping roles. It explores the activities of counselling, coaching and mentoring, highlighting the differences between each and identifying the shared features. Chapter 2 introduces helpers to a particular 'model' or approach for engaging in helping relationships with clients. It suggests an integrative way of working, whereby helpers strive to build a relationship of trust based on empathic listening, a non-judgemental approach, and a genuine engagement in the process, whilst drawing on skills and strategies from goal-directed ways of working towards positive change with clients. Chapters 3, 4 and 5 are concerned with the skills of helping. Chapter 3 explores the foundation skills in detail: skills of listening, reflection, summarising and questioning. Chapter 4 focuses on advanced skills and techniques including the use of challenge and information sharing in the helping context, whilst Chapter 5 considers how skills are used in the helping relationship to ensure that a contract is established, agendas are agreed, and the work remains goal focused. Chapters 6 to 8 introduce some key concepts that are central to helping practice – reflection, ethical working and working with diversity – whilst Chapter 9 encourages readers to think about how their work will be supported in supervision.

Each chapter begins with a clear set of objectives, setting out what will be addressed. Opportunities are provided throughout for readers to engage with activities in order to reflect on key questions, develop their skills further, and apply theory to practice. Case studies, testimonies and vignettes enable contextualised illustration and deeper understanding. At the end of each chapter, additional reading is signposted to deepen readers' understanding further. The case studies in Part II are referenced throughout Part I and should be used as examples of 'real-life' practice.

Part II

Practitioners in a range of helping roles – counsellors, coaches, mentors and others – have provided examples of real clients (all anonymised) to enable further contextualisation, reflection and deeper understanding for readers. This section can be used in a 'stand-alone' capacity, or in conjunction with Part I, where these examples of actual helping practice are referred to throughout. The case studies used demonstrate the breadth of helping roles: from a life-coach in private practice to a teacher working in a hospital school; from a care manager in a residential home to a telephone helpline counsellor. At the end of each case study, readers are invited to reflect on the skills and approaches being used by the helper, whilst considering the challenges of engaging with each client. Finally, readers are invited to consider their own response to the helping roles identified. Are these areas of helping practice that appeal?

What follows is an introduction to professional helping. The rest of this introduction offers the opportunity for readers to begin to engage fully with the text – to digest, reflect, engage with activities, and develop thinking about what professional helping means in practice.

What does 'helping' mean?

It is important that those who decide to enter the helping professions have a clear understanding as to what 'helping' means. The concept of helping may appear obvious, but the definition of helping within the context of a counselling, coaching or mentoring role is complex. Reflection on and understanding of the meaning of helping is important in enabling individuals to decide whether or not to enter this area of work. Hawkins and Shohet (2000), writing about the role of the helper, suggest that:

> it is essential for all those in the helping professions to reflect honestly on the complex mixture of motives that have led them to choose their current profession and role. (2000: 8)

The purpose of this introduction, in part, is to offer readers the opportunity to consider and respond to Hawkins and Shohet's assertion that helpers should 'reflect honestly' on their motivation for entering this field of endeavour. If you are new to helping or are at a point where you are considering working in the broad remit of the helping professions, what follows will clarify some of the key aspects of helping relationships and assist you to reflect on your own motivation for your career choice. If you are already engaged in a role within the helping professions, this introduction will offer you the opportunity to reflect on the purpose and focus of the relationships you establish with clients, and act as a reminder as to what you are working to achieve.

The helping relationship

Most of us, if asked, would perceive ourselves as being helpful individuals. It is unlikely that many would describe themselves as unhelpful people. But the meaning of 'being helpful' depends, to a large extent, on the context in which the help is sought. The reason for needing help in the first place dictates the kind of help that is required. People seek help from counsellors, coaches and mentors for a range of reasons; but whatever the reason for needing support, 'fixing', 'leading' and 'mending' are not words that are normally used to describe counselling, coaching and mentoring relationships. These helping professions – and those who work within them – do not purport to have answers to their clients' issues and difficulties, and neither is their role as a 'helper' concerned with telling someone what to do or even doing it for them. Rather, where the help required is psychological, emotional or behavioural (as is the case in counselling, coaching and mentoring relationships), it is the role of the helper to walk alongside rather than lead, to enable rather than control, to assist rather than fix. Reid and Fielding offer a simple and accurate definition of helping relationships when they write about working with young people. They suggest:

> A helping relationship enables the young person to move towards their personal goals and to strengthen their ability to manage issues or problems in their lives. It is a collaborative relationship characterized by flexibility on the part of the professional helper in identifying and meeting the individual needs of the young person. (2007: 10)

Whitmore, defining a coaching relationship, emphasises the development of self-efficacy as central in helping relationships, suggesting that this kind of helping is about

> unlocking people's potential to maximize their own performance. It is helping them to learn, rather than teaching them. (2009: 11)

My own, simple and straightforward definition of a helping relationship, which can be applied equally to counselling, coaching and mentoring contexts, is as follows:

A helper engages with and works alongside a client to assist them to identify their issues, challenges and needs, to reflect on and explore these issues, and to enable their client to work towards positive change.

This definition highlights the need for engagement in a relationship and suggests that it is the client who has the responsibility for decision making whilst the helper works collaboratively alongside them. Furthermore, the concept of change as being central to helping is made explicit – change in thoughts, feelings or behaviour, where decisions have had to be taken and actions carried out. The case studies in Part II each serve to illustrate this definition in practice. Each 'helper' describes the supportive and enabling relationships they have formed with their clients, whereby clients work hard to identify their issues, explore options, make decisions and take control of their own lives. In the testimony below, Charmaine, a student on a counselling degree programme, explains her understanding of the helping relationship in client work.

Case study: Charmaine (trainee counsellor)

I applied to train as a counsellor because I knew I wanted to help people. When I was interviewed for a place on the course, I was asked what I thought helping meant, and what I saw as the role of the counsellor. I think that I responded by saying that helping is about 'giving advice' to people when they are experiencing difficulties in their lives – or something like that – and it's come as a surprise to me on my course that counsellors actually *don't* advise their clients about what they should do. It's been one of the most difficult things to get my head around really. I can see now that I, as a counsellor, can't expect to know a client better than they know themselves, and therefore *they* are best placed to make decisions about their lives. I still find it hard, though, when I think that they're doing something wrong. I just want to tell them to do something else instead, something better. But I'm learning all about being non-judgemental, empathic and congruent, and although this is hard to understand, it's helping me to see that I really don't know best – even if I think I do!

Charmaine describes a common misconception concerning helping relationships, namely that ultimately the helper knows what is best for the client. She goes on to make reference to empathy, congruence and unconditional positive regard – the core conditions central to working with clients. These conditions are explored in some depth in Chapter 2, and understanding and applying the core conditions forms the bedrock of most helping relationships. Charmaine is learning that every person she will work with is unique, with their own personal experiences, feelings, physical characteristics, aptitudes, cultural influences, upbringing, beliefs, values and so on. It is this uniqueness that makes it impossible for someone who does not share those characteristics and experiences – and no one does – to tell someone else what they should do for the best. And neither is the concept of doing what is 'best' straightforward.

Those who are drawn to work in the helping professions are attracted to this kind of role for a reason. Some might describe the work as a 'calling', whilst others may perceive it, albeit unconsciously, as a way to heal themselves. Whatever your perspective, the helping professions are so much more than 'just a job', and motivation for working in a helping role should be examined before a commitment to the work is made.

Motivation for helping

Hawkins and Shohet write honestly and thoughtfully about the motivation for helping. They focus on the positives whilst being mindful of what they describe as the 'shadow side' of helping: the need to validate ourselves, 'heal' our own pain, or simply view ourselves through the lens of our clients. They explain how many people are likely to respond to the question 'Why helping?':

> For most of us the answer to the question of 'why' would include the wish to care for, cure, to heal – an attraction to the 'healer-patient archetype'. Alongside this, however, may be a hidden need for power, both in surrounding oneself with people worse off, and being able to direct parts of the lives of people who need help. (2000: 11)

It can be tricky to reflect honestly on what attracts us to the work of professional helping. There are probably a range of reasons for being interested in the complexity of other people's lives. Human beings are fascinating creatures; no one person is the same as another so the work is never repetitive or dull, and positive outcomes can be powerful and emotional events – for the helper as well as the client. But there are also likely to be power-related needs, unresolved emotional or psychological issues, and possibly even interdependency concerns on the part of the helper. For professional accreditation in some helping professions, trainees are required to engage in their own personal therapy. An understanding of who we are at a deep and reflexive level, and, in particular, acknowledgement of our own unresolved issues, can be helpful in illuminating our thoughts and feelings when we engage with clients. Of course, most helpers in professional practice will be supervised regularly. The supervisory relationship (discussed in full in Chapter 9) offers helpers their own 'space' to reflect on themselves in relation to the client with whom they are working.

Activity: Why do I want to be a helper?

Write down a list of reasons that attract you to work in the helping professions. Come back to the list after a day or so and reflect on your motivation. How much of what drives you is about the needs of others? How much is about meeting your own need to be 'useful', 'needed' or 'powerful' in someone else's life?

Everyone who is honest and open about their motivation for helping – counselling, coaching or mentoring – will know that at some level the work is meeting a need within themselves. This is not, in itself, a 'bad' thing, but it is important that helpers have a raised self-awareness of what is 'in it for me' to ensure that their work remains client focused at all times. Hawkins and Shohet explain:

> As part of our training we are taught to pay attention to client needs, and it is often difficult to focus on our own needs. It is even considered selfish, self-indulgent. Yet our needs are there nonetheless. They are there, we believe, *in our very motives for the work we do.* (2000: 13, emphasis in original)

Hawkins and Shohet go on to reassure us that, in spite of the 'shadow-side' of helping, the desire to support is fundamental, and the basic need to heal is central to human nature – whether a professional helper, a construction worker, a banker or a circus performer. Any of the above are likely to go to the aid of someone they see in distress or pain, as a basic act of human kindness. But it is a deep interest in the lives of others – their motivations, experiences, thoughts, behaviour and feelings – that sets apart those who embark on a career in the helping professions from other kinds of work-related activity.

Characteristics of a professional helping relationship

We can almost certainly identify times in our lives where we have been helpful to friends, family members or colleagues. We may have listened, offered emotional support, advised, cajoled, instructed and so on. Although these activities may have helped at the time, they are not the same as professional helping. The main reason for this is that the help offered would not have been impartial. In other words you, as a friend, family member or colleague, would be 'in the mix' – having a personal view grounded in the perspective from which the relationship derives, but not necessarily the 'whole picture'. Furthermore, it is likely that the recipient of your help (your friend, family member or colleague) would not have been completely open and honest with you. There may have been elements of their situation that they chose to keep hidden from you because they would not want to jeopardise their relationship with you or risk your disapproval. Although they may have since told you how much you helped, your helping would have come with elements of your own agenda attached, and it is likely to be based on the significant features, but not all, of the story. Kevin, a relationship counsellor, explains as follows.

Case study: Kevin – helping relationships with friends

Most of my friends know that I'm a relationship counsellor and they understand that this does not mean I solve other people's problems and sort out lives. And especially not theirs! Nevertheless when a very good friend asked to talk to me, as he had found out that his wife was having an affair and had said she wanted to leave him, I agreed to meet up for a chat. I found our meeting difficult and painful. And I suspect that he did too. I was feeling as shocked as he was. I'm a good friend with his wife too, and I felt 'let down' and 'betrayed' in a small part, because I had known nothing about her affair. We also regularly spend weekends together – my friend and his wife, and me and my partner – and I was all too aware that I would inevitably lose this dimension of our relationship. In other words, I was 'in the mix' and was unable to focus entirely on my friend. Furthermore, of course, there would have been elements of my friend's relationship with his wife that he might have found hard to talk about with me – an old friend who was also friends with his wife. This was never going to be a particularly helpful intervention, and I left feeling exhausted and depressed, as I had tried to listen and not interject by burdening my friend with my own feelings. I'm pleased to say that my friend and his wife are now receiving couples counselling. My partner and I meet up with them both regularly, and although there has been an inevitable shift in our relationship, we have talked about the ways in which things have changed and are each clear about the boundaries of our friendship: we are there for each other, but I am not able to offer therapy.

Professional helping relationships should be based upon key criteria:

- *Impartiality* – the helper should not normally know (outside the therapeutic relationship) the person they are working to help. The focus is on the client: their needs, their issues, their life. The counselling relationship is the 'pure' definition of this, whereby little or nothing is known about the counsellor. The mentoring relationship, by contrast, may be less rigid and formal in that sense, although impartiality to the mentee remains paramount.
- *Openness* – a relationship is built and maintained whereby the client can be open, transparent and honest about their thoughts, feelings and actions without fear of judgement, disapproval or ridicule.
- *Trust* – the client trusts the helper to 'contain' their story without breaking confidentiality. The client trusts that the helper is working with them for positive change. The helper would never abuse this trust, and this is central to working ethically within the helping professions (see Chapter 7 for a more detailed introduction to ethical working).
- *Client-centred* – adherence to the core conditions of empathy, congruence and unconditional positive regard, whereby the helper works hard to understand their client's frame of reference; is genuine and 'real' in the relationship; and values their client as a unique human being (see Chapter 2 for a fuller explanation of these core conditions).

Meeting these criteria is not always straightforward, even in a professional helping context, particularly where the role of the helper is not solely focused on counselling, coaching or mentoring. The probation officer's case study in Part II explains how her role, although primarily concerned with help and support, must also address issues of reoffending and criminal behaviour and, where necessary, attend to convictions and application of punishments. The hospital teacher's case study in Part II also demonstrates the challenges that can arise when 'helping' is not necessarily the sole function of the professional role. The writer describes how his role as a teacher, working in a hospital, primarily attends to the learning needs of his patients, but that helping is often central in responding to the needs of the sick children and young people with whom he works.

As explained more fully in Chapter 1, helping is not the same as giving advice, telling someone what to do, instructing, directing, insisting, informing and so on. All of the aforementioned activities suggest a power dynamic whereby the helper is an expert who possesses all the answers. The most important facts of which the helper must be aware are that they do not hold any answers, they are not in control of someone else's life, and their role is to *em*power – not to exert – power.

Activity: How effective a helper am I?

First, go back to your definition of helping from the initial activity in this chapter. On rereading is there anything that you would like to add or amend? Second, take a moment to reflect deeply on the challenges that will (or do already) face you as a professional helper. It might help to talk this through with a friend. Try to be as honest as you can about your own motivation and the aspects of helping that you are likely to find difficult. Ask yourself these questions:

- How challenging might I find it to 'walk alongside' rather than direct?
- How often do I think that I know what is best for others?
- How do I feel when others ignore my advice?
- Who has directed my life and made important decisions for me?

Every professional helper at some time struggles with their role. That is why supervision is so important – to work through, reflect on and learn from the struggles. The good helper is one who admits the challenges they face and works hard to understand them. The helper who constantly defends their practice, is not able to face the 'shadow-side' of the work, and justifies their interventions without questioning is likely to struggle to meet the conditions and qualities for effective helping.

The role of the helper is not about imposing one's own view, but about encouraging our clients to identify their issues and needs and make changes in their lives. Reid and Fielding (2007) call this emphasis on change with clients 'moving on'. They make the point that the work of a helping professional should be finite; in other words clients should be enabled to move on so that ultimately they do not require the help of professionals in order to manage aspects of their lives effectively.

Attributes of an effective helper

The *attributes* of helping are different to the *characteristics* of a helping relationship as detailed earlier in this introduction. Rather, attributes are qualities that anyone wanting to enter the helping professions and take on an effective helping role should hold. These attributes are as follows:

- A belief that individuals have the ability to make positive changes in their lives.
- An interest in people – their lives, their complexities and their challenges.

- A basic respect for others.
- An ability to listen to others.
- An ability to build trusting relationships.
- A desire to know themselves better.
- An ability to reflect on themselves – their own thoughts, feelings, behaviours, beliefs, values and experiences.

These attributes are fundamental to effective helping, and those who hold these attributes (with training) are likely to be able to develop the skills and learn the techniques necessary to engage with others and assist them to move on. The skills and techniques can be taught and developed, but the attributes detailed above are not so easily learned: they are part of who we are, as people. Not everyone possesses these attributes, and those who do not are unlikely to be interested in working in a helping role.

Activity: Attributes for effective helping

Reflect on the bullet-point list of key attributes detailed above. What are your own personal responses to these attributes? Can you give examples which demonstrate that you possess each of these attributes? Are there attributes on this list that you find challenging, that you are not sure are fully developed yet? How might you begin to develop these further?

Although the list above defines a range of key attributes that are essential to effective helping, it may not necessarily be that you are able to confidently tick off every item on the list. This is unsurprising. Factors like self-reflection require practice, and although the basic desire and interest in ourselves should be evident, the tools for understanding ourselves better also have to be learned. Chapter 6 focuses on reflective practice and this will offer much greater insight into how this attribute might be developed further.

Summary

I began this introduction by setting out a rationale for this text and recommending ways in which the book could be used. I suggest that what is covered here is likely to be helpful for those who are in the very early stages of considering a career in the helping professions, as well as for those who have already embarked on training programmes or are even currently employed in an area of helping practice.

For those who have yet to engage in professional helping relationships, you should now be clearer about what this type of relationship looks like: what it sets out to achieve and, importantly, what it is not. For those in training or practice, you will have had the opportunity to reflect further on what a professional helping relationship means and to consider your own practice; to what extent do you meet the criteria for effective helping? How finely honed are your personal helping attributes?

Now you should be ready to embark upon reading the book and begin to develop further the key skills, techniques and knowledge necessary for effective helping.

PART I
THEORY, APPROACHES AND SKILLS

1

HELPING ROLES AND PROFESSIONS
DEFINING THE TERMS

Chapter objectives: Readers will have the opportunity to …

- define the term 'helping professions';
- explain the key features of counselling, coaching and mentoring relationships;
- identify the professional contexts in which counselling, coaching and mentoring take place;
- consider the shared elements of each discipline;
- identify the differences and distinctions in approach.

Introduction

The expression 'helping professions' has become ubiquitous and is used to describe a range of roles identified within a broad spectrum of professional contexts, from psychotherapists to learning mentors, social care support workers to life-coaches, and careers counsellors to paramedics. The concept of a 'helping relationship' has also gained momentum, and terms such as 'therapy', 'counselling', 'coaching', 'mentoring' and 'guidance' are often used interchangeably to describe the nature and features of such a relationship. But what is meant by the term 'helping professions'? And what does a helping relationship look like? What do the activities of counselling, coaching and mentoring set out to achieve? Are their aims shared – or are there distinctive elements to each approach?

This first chapter sets out to define and demystify some of the key terms which will be used throughout the text. It begins by establishing what is meant by the broad term 'helping professions' and then goes on to focus on the one-to-one helping relationship, by defining and examining the aim, purpose and nature of counselling, coaching and mentoring activities. It is important to note that the meanings of these terms are not universally agreed, but heavily contested. There are practitioners, academics and researchers in each of the three fields presented above who argue vehemently that the activities are distinct; they strive for different outcomes, are based on diverse – sometimes conflicting – theoretical perspectives, and make use of what could be termed 'incompatible' skills and techniques. However, there are also practitioners, academics and researchers who consider that there are shared features, approaches, skills and techniques in these helping fields, and that perhaps these common aspects are greater than the distinctions that set each activity apart. I do not presume to have a definitive answer, but will strive to present a coherent definition of each activity – counselling, coaching and mentoring – and invite you to reach your own conclusions. We do know, though, that the helping professions are a growth field, and a number of new practitioner roles have emerged in recent years: roles such as mentor, care support worker, pastoral manager, life-coach and so on. These job titles are familiar to us now, but have only become so very recently.

A range of case studies, activities and reflection opportunities will be presented throughout the chapter (as in all the chapters in this book). In addition, the real-life practitioner scenarios presented in Part II will contextualise the contents of Part I and enable a greater depth and breadth of understanding about the helping professions, the roles involved, and the ways in which helping skills and processes are applied.

The helping professions

Egan (2007), in his seminal text *The Skilled Helper*, uses the term 'helping' in a generic sense to describe those who use counselling and helping skills as a central element in their work. This includes counsellors, psychotherapists and so on, but also encapsulates other professionals – mentors, support workers, paramedics, teachers and social workers, for example – who are not necessarily engaged in therapeutic interventions, but are working alongside others (patients, pupils, clients) in a supportive and helping context. Nelson-Jones makes a distinction between counsellors and helpers, citing helpers as 'paraprofessional or quasi-counsellors, those who use counselling skills as part of other primary roles, those engaged in voluntary counselling and helping, and those who participate in peer helping or support networks' (2012: 6). Cameron suggests something slightly different, going further by offering a more comprehensive insight into what constitutes a 'helping profession':

> The helping professions – social work, health and welfare work and community work, to include just a few fields of endeavour – comprise an essential field of practice in most countries. Practitioners interact with clients across the full range of health, family, youth, justice, housing and education service sectors in most societies. (2008: 2)

Activity

Take a moment to focus on a particular institution that you think might employ 'helpers'. It could be a school, a hospital, a care home, a prison or a social services department – or somewhere else which has the primary concern of working in some capacity with people. Now make a list of all the roles in that institution which you think have 'helping' as their focus.

I am sure that you were able to name a number of roles that included helping as their primary focus. For example, in the case of schools or other education establishments today, you are likely to come across learning mentors, school counsellors, learning support assistants, teaching assistants, pastoral support workers, pastoral managers, educational social workers, and others whose primary task is to support children and young people in their learning and more broadly in managing their young lives. But would you consider that teachers also engage in helping relationships with their pupils? The testimonial below, from Carly, an English teacher in a secondary school, offers an enlightening insight.

Case study: Carly (secondary-school teacher)

I work as an English teacher, which means that I undertake all the tasks that you would expect. I engage with students through a range of learning activities: I set them work tasks, mark their course work, help to prepare them for their exams, and generally support their learning in relation to my subject, English.

I also have responsibility for a tutor group – students who I have worked with since they first joined the school and will stay with until they (or I!) leave.

(Continued)

(Continued)

We meet every day for tutorial time and during these sessions, over the years, I have been approached by students wishing to disclose a range of challenging issues: from describing their experiences of domestic violence to disclosing news of an unplanned pregnancy. In a number of cases, I know that I have been the first adult that these young people have spoken to about quite intimate and private aspects of their lives. I think that is probably because over the years we have built a relationship of trust, and they feel safe enough to share their problems with me. Of course, there was nothing in my teacher training that prepared me for this aspect of my job. I feel honoured that pupils feel able to confide in me, but I'm not always sure where I can go with these problems, or what to do about them. I'm certainly not a trained counsellor!

Carly highlights the tension that many professionals face – doctors, social workers, health workers, care workers, even small employers supporting a staff team, for example – whereby the role of counsellor, coach or mentor is not the central element of their function, but nevertheless they often find themselves engaging with clients or colleagues to offer emotional support as well as practical help. Usually they have had very little training in the use of helping skills and approaches, and simply do the best they can in each individual case. Kelly, a senior paramedic, highlights this issue in her testimony below.

Case study: Kelly (senior paramedic)

I was prepared for the clinical elements of the role of paramedic and feel confident in my medical practice. What I was less prepared for – and I know that many paramedics share this concern – is the emotional and psychological aspects of the work, where we are often dealing with anxious and distraught patients and relatives; elderly, frail people who may be frightened and confused; and friends and family members of patients who may have gone through a very traumatic experience. In many cases, it is the paramedic who deals directly with these issues, as they are the first person at the scene. Of course, our work is to care for the health of our patients first and foremost, but that doesn't take away from the fact that we are also working in relationships that require elements of broader help and support.

Kelly's testimony, like Carly's, demonstrates that many professionals in roles that are not identified primarily as counsellors, coaches or mentors nevertheless engage in some kind of supportive relationship where they use helping skills to assist their clients, patients, pupils or employees to manage challenging issues in their lives.

So, in order to define the term 'helping professions', we may have to look further than naming a role in an organisation that is defined solely as 'therapeutic', and think more broadly about practitioners who use the skills of helping as an element of their function, which would not necessarily be assumed from their job title.

Reflection point

Take a moment to think about your own work role – or the role that you would like to undertake in the future. How far would you describe this as belonging primarily to a counselling, coaching or mentoring profession, or rather an organisation where you use helping skills as a key element of your work? How far would you define yourself (or like to define yourself in the future) as a counsellor, coach or mentor first and foremost – or as something else? Try to establish how many of your working hours are taken up in engaging in helping relationships (or how much of your time you would like to devote to this in the future).

Even if you do not necessarily see yourself in a helping profession or role, the use of helping skills as an aspect of everyday life can be invaluable. Culley and Bond ask:

> How can we help someone when the obvious ways do not seem to work? How can we help others solve problems better? How can we assist someone to communicate their point of view better? These are common challenges for us in work, especially in health and social care and education. They are also everyday challenges with friends, colleagues and sometimes in chance encounters with strangers. (2011: ix)

They go on to suggest that knowledge of counselling and helping skills can assist us all to engage more actively in a range of different contexts, be it in work or in our private lives. If, then, we can identify a range of different helping roles, how do we know whether these can be termed 'counsellor', 'coach' or 'mentor'? Are these activities interchangeable? Do they effectively mean the same thing? Do they require a different skill-set? And what about the knowledge needed to be effective counsellors, coaches and mentors? The introduction to this book examined the key features of helping relationships (the skills and qualities needed to be an effective helper) and these will be explored in greater depth in

Chapters 2, 3, 4 and 5. But we will take some time now to focus on the most commonly known helping roles – counsellor, coach and mentor – to attempt to reach a shared definition of each.

Activity

Before we explore, define and attempt to demystify the terms, take a moment to write down your own definitions of 'counsellor', 'coach' and 'mentor'.

You will have the opportunity to return to your definitions after reading this section, which sets out to describe each activity clearly.

Counselling

Counsellors are employed in a range of contexts: health, education, the voluntary and community sectors, and private practice. They often develop specialisms in terms of the issues they deal with, for example bereavement, addiction, working with young people, relationships and so on. Feltham offers a broad definition of the purpose of counselling, which he describes as

> mainly, though not exclusively, listening-and-talking-based methods of addressing psychological and psychosomatic problems and change, including deep and prolonged human suffering, situational dilemmas, crises and developmental needs, and aspirations towards the realisation of human potential. In contrast to bio-medical approaches, the psychological therapies operate largely without medication or other physical interventions and may be concerned not only with mental health but with spiritual, philosophical, social and other aspects of living. Professional forms of counselling and psychotherapy are based on formal training which encompasses attention to pertinent theory, clinical and/or micro-skills development, the personal development/ theory of the trainee, and supervised practice. (2012: 3)

The point is made here that counselling attends to psychological and psychosomatic disturbances. Its primary concern is the emotional lives of clients, helping them to understand their thoughts, feelings and behaviours. But counselling aims for more than simply exploring and reaching an enhanced understanding of clients' lives. It not only focuses on exploring these 'disturbances' – although the exploration is a very important aspect – but also attends equally to working towards change, if and when clients feel able to make adaptations in their lives. Counselling is therefore a purposeful relationship that aims for some kind of positive change. Feltham also draws our attention to the need for an appropriately trained and effectively supervised counselling workforce. All counsellors undertake rigorous training which helps them to develop knowledge and skills in a range of important areas, depending on the particular theoretical orientation in which they practise. The concept of 'theoretical orientation' will be explained later in this book but, for now, it can be defined as the particular counselling approach that is adopted, for example person-centred, cognitive behavioural or psychodynamic. An integrative approach draws on a range of orientations and adopts a particular model within which different approaches can be integrated as appropriate. As well as undergoing thorough and in-depth professional training, all counsellors who are registered members of the British Association for Counselling and Psychotherapy (BACP) and who also practise counselling are required to engage in their own professional supervision. This means that counsellors have regular opportunities to reflect on their practice and ensure that they are keeping themselves and their clients safe in the counselling process.

There is an on-going debate about the distinctions between counselling and psychotherapy, and although space does not allow an in-depth exploration of these perceived differences here, Claringbull provides a useful and pragmatic response to the question of the differences between counselling and psychotherapy:

> The answer to the 'what's in a name' puzzle is simple: there are NO differences. If you are a professional – and that includes all the personal therapists – who is trying to help somebody with emotional, personal or mental health problems, then you are a psychological therapist and practising what today are often called the talking therapies. (2010: 4)

The purpose of counselling can be summarised as follows. Counsellors focus on:

- building a relationship of trust – by engaging actively with each and every client, and providing a safe and confidential space in which to listen to their stories;
- enabling clients to express their feelings freely and openly without judgement – offering a cathartic experience;
- working therapeutically with clients – encouraging their clients to focus on and understand better the tensions, conflicts and challenges in their lives in relation to thoughts, feelings and behaviour;
- taking an empathic and non-judgemental approach – working hard to understand each client's circumstances from their frame of reference, and accepting each client unconditionally, without judgement;
- being 'real' in their relationships with clients – the counsellor develops an in-depth understanding of 'self' within each counselling

relationship, knowing what issues may trigger a particular response in the counsellor and where this response resides; put simply, developing as a reflexive and reflective practitioner;

- assisting clients to work towards developing a fuller understanding of themselves – enabling clients to focus on and explore their thoughts, feelings and behaviours and gain a greater depth of understanding about their motivations and the underlying causes of their issues;
- enabling clients to work towards change – working with clients to begin to look forward and consider options and strategies for making positive changes in their lives, in relation to thoughts, feelings and behaviours.

Rajesh, a relationship counsellor, summarises his role and reflects on what he is setting out to achieve in his work with clients.

Case study: Rajesh (relationship counsellor)

I've been working as a relationship counsellor for ten years now. It's funny, but I wouldn't describe myself as an experienced counsellor. Each client and each piece of work feels so new and so different. If you're asking me what counselling is all about and what I do … hmm … that's a tricky one. I suppose that I'd say that first and foremost I'm offering a safe space to my clients – whether I'm seeing a couple or just one person – I'm offering them an opportunity to be listened to, without judgement, and to say things that may have been previously unspoken, and to feel things that may challenge or even frighten them in some way. When people say to me 'Oh, all you counsellors do is sit and listen and nod!' I have to smile to myself. If only! Sitting with someone's pain is exhausting. And finding the right words to help them to explore that pain is a fine art – and I'm sure that I don't always get it right. But the most difficult thing for me is knowing that I can't solve their problems. I'm not there to advise or recommend, but I am there to help clients to find their own solutions. And sometimes the solutions can be just as challenging as the original problem.

Rajesh reminds us that counselling is not the same as advising. The role of the counsellor is not to dictate, recommend or even advise clients on what is best, but rather to enable clients to share their stories in a safe and non-judgemental space and identify the options and evaluate the actions that are best for them, in their circumstances, in their lives.

Activity

Look at the list of statements below. What are your thoughts? Do you agree that these responses in a counselling context could be unhelpful? What is your reasoning?
Counselling is *not*:

- Giving advice – 'In your situation you should probably ...'
- Telling someone what to do – 'You must make sure you ...'
- Telling someone what you would do – 'If I were you I'd ...'
- Telling someone that the same thing has happened to you – 'I know just what you're going through. The same thing happened to me, and this is what I did ...'
- Reassuring someone that everything will be OK – 'Don't worry. I'm sure it will all be fine ...It'll all work out in the end.'
- Interpreting someone's thoughts, feelings and behaviours – 'I think that you do this because ...'
- Showing sympathy – 'You poor old thing ...'

Of course, the reason that people choose a career in the helping professions is because they want to help! But helping (and counselling) doesn't mean telling people what to do. If we reflect on our own lives, we will probably come to the realisation that most of the significant decisions we have made have been made by us – not by someone else telling us what to do. Rajesh stresses the difficulty of sitting with someone's pain rather than trying to offer a quick fix or tell them that everything will be fine. We cannot possibly know if all will be well in the future for our clients, and therefore counsellors must maintain their integrity and not attempt the unachievable – 'solving' the problems of others.

Geldard and Geldard summarise the purpose of counselling elegantly:

> A major goal of the counselling process therefore needs to be to help clients change. Clients need to be able to make changes in the way they think and/or the things they do, so that they are less likely to repeat patterns of thinking and behaving which lead to negative consequences for them. *Effective counselling helps people change.* (2005: 9, emphasis in original)

Activity

Take a moment to read Case Study 7 in Part II. This contributor works as a counsellor and coach therapist. How far does her work fit within the definition of counselling set out here?

So, counselling is about the emotional and psychological well-being of clients. It is focused on exploring the presenting problem and working towards greater understanding and, ultimately, positive change. What about coaching and mentoring – do these activities work towards the same goals, or is there a different focus and purpose?

Coaching

Coaching is a relatively new and rapidly expanding sector. We have probably all heard the term 'life-coach', and this may bring to mind images of a wealthy, middle-class individual experiencing a mid-life crisis and going to someone for help in finding a new direction in their lives. This is an unhelpful and stereotypical view of life-coaching, but nevertheless resonates to a degree. The purpose of coaching is goal orientated and tends to focus on aspects of our personal and professional lives and the balance between them. Unlike counselling, where people often present in distress, with a deep-rooted, complex issue or 'problem', coaching is based on the premise of 'enabling' or 'maximising' potential in our lives. Van Nieuwerburgh (2014) suggests that the following definitions provide a useful insight. Downey (2003: 21) offers a simple explanation of coaching as 'the art of facilitating the performance, learning and development of another'. Whitmore (2009: 11) agrees that coaching is all about 'unlocking people's potential to maximise their own performance. It is helping them to learn rather than teaching them.' De Haan (2008: 19) concurs, explaining that 'coaching is a method of work-related learning that relies primarily on one-to-one conversations.' Cox, Bachkirova and Clutterbuck (2014: 1) go further, suggesting that coaching is 'a human development process that involves structured, focused interaction and the use of appropriate strategies, tools and techniques to promote desirable and sustainable change for the benefit of the coachee and potentially for other stakeholders'. There are clues here in the terminology used to define coaching. Terms like 'performance', 'work-related', 'development' and 'learning' suggest a particular focus to these coaching interventions that is, perhaps, different to the counselling relationship. Van Nieuwerburgh (2014) goes on to suggest that coaching is all about empowerment, particularly in relation to learning, growth and personal and professional development.

Unlike counselling, the coaching profession has, until recently, been largely unregulated. Coaching training programmes and courses have been relatively scarce and the rigorous codes of ethics and principles which underpin counselling work have not been so prominent in coaching practice, although that is set to change. A gradual awareness of the importance of coaching and its relevance as a core activity within the helping professions has been recognised. The BACP, for example, has a coaching division and includes information about courses and programmes with a coaching focus in their list of accredited training routes. Furthermore, it is planned that coaches will have access to the BACP revised *Ethical Framework* (2015), which will include practice guidance for coaching. So let us try to define coaching in a little more detail.

Van Nieuwerburgh (2014) suggests that coaching involves three key elements:

- A 'managed' conversation that takes place between two people (a coach and a coachee) and focuses on the issues brought by the coachee in a safe and supportive environment.
- A process that aims to encourage, enable and support changes in behaviours or ways of thinking that are achievable and, importantly, sustainable for the coachee.
- A process that focuses on learning and development; this could be in relation to work practices, professional training, work–life balance, or career development.

There appear to be 'shared' factors here between counselling and coaching. Both stress the need for a safe and supportive relationship, and both work towards change. The key differences here are the focus of the work (as already established, the work of a coach is primarily concerned with personal and professional development, often in a professional, career-related context) and, perhaps, the depth in which any emotional and psychological issues are explored. In the case study below, Carl talks about his practice as a coach in a large organisation.

Case study: Carl (coach in an organisation)

I've been working for a large multinational organisation for three years. I was the first person to be appointed to this post in the UK, and I think it came about initially because the organisation was concerned about staff retention and progression. I'm actually based in the HR department, but my job is different to what we would normally think of as human resources work. I've coached a whole range of different people within the organisation. The senior and middle managers have regular, programmed coaching sessions, as does anyone who is approaching retirement. Anyone in the organisation can request a coaching session and often individuals are referred to me following their appraisals with

(Continued)

(Continued)

managers, where they have indicated a desire to progress further within the organisation or look for a new professional direction. My coaching practice focuses very much on work-related issues – be it thinking about changes in work, developing better work practices, moving into different professional areas, or moving out of the workplace altogether. I'm often faced with clients who are struggling to get their work–life balance right. That's probably the issue I deal with most, to be honest. I help people to think about what they want, and how they can get it, but I will always refer people on if I feel that they need more in-depth psychological or therapeutic support, which is not my role.

Carl is very clear here about the boundaries of his role – where he 'stops' and a counsellor might take over. This is important and is an on-going challenge for Carl in his work as a coach. Unlike a counsellor, Carl is not required to have regular supervision, and therefore has to make important decisions about his practice (referrals, for example) using his own skills of reflexivity and reflection.

Activity

Look at the list of statements below. What are your thoughts? Do you agree that these responses in a coaching context could be unhelpful? What is your reasoning?

- 'I think you need to leave the job you're working in. You're obviously unhappy there!'
- 'Why don't you go for promotion? You've been stuck in that same old job for years.'
- 'When I was working under pressure like you, I made the decision to stop checking my e-mails at home. That's something I'd advise you to do too.'
- 'Have you thought about trying something else? What about training as a nurse, or a banker, or a florist?'

It should not be assumed that coaching is any more about 'telling people what to do' than counselling. The coach is skilled in active listening and questioning techniques, and knows that it is their clients who are the experts in their own lives and who must find the solutions that work for them – just as with their counselling colleagues. That said, the work is goal focused and a coach will often work at a faster pace than a counsellor, with perhaps a more explicitly defined goal-orientated focus and, possibly, fewer one-to-one sessions.

Activity

Take a moment to read Case Study 2, in Part II. How does this example of a coach's work fit with your understanding of coaching practice?

To summarise our understanding so far, Garvey, Stokes and Megginson suggest that the term 'coaching' is

> used extensively in business environments. This is either in the form of internal line manager coaches or with the use of external and paid coaches. These are often positioned as 'executive coaches'. Life-coaching is almost exclusively linked to paid practice. Coaching is still associated with performance improvement of a specific kind related to a job role, but it is also increasingly linked to leadership development, transition and change and generally developing a focus for the future. (2014: 27)

It should not be assumed, however, that coaches operate only in 'business' or private-practice settings. Education and health are both professions where the practice of coaching is recognised as being helpful.

Where counselling and coaching are considered to be relatively 'formal' activities – with clearly established agreements around appointment times, for example, and a boundaried nature in the relationship between counsellors, coaches and their clients – the activity of mentoring suggests a slightly different focus in the nature of the relationship.

Mentoring

The *Oxford English Dictionary* offers an interesting definition of a mentor, given the context of this book. It suggests that a mentor is 'an experienced and trusted counsellor'. Although use of the term 'counsellor' is interesting, it serves to muddy the water a little, but it is the emphasis on 'experience' and 'trust' that is the clue to what is at the heart of a mentoring relationship. Pask and Joy (2007) describe the role of a mentor in clear terms as someone who simply helps someone else to think things through, and this is certainly true. A mentoring relationship, like coaching (and unlike counselling) is often related to the workplace or to education. Learning mentors can be found in almost all schools, colleges, universities and other educational establishments, whilst mentors are also employed in many workplaces.

Activity

Imagine that you are currently employed (it really does not matter what type of work you are doing; let's use a fast-food customer assistant as an example). Your manager asks you to act as a mentor to a new member of staff. What do you imagine your job will involve? Jot down your thoughts.

It is likely that you identified activities which would enable your new colleague to understand better what their job involves and the processes and procedures involved therein. You probably established that this would be a fairly 'informal' relationship and that your new colleague would be able to talk to you and question you about issues in the workplace as they arose, rather than wait for a formal 'mentoring appointment'. The informal nature of the mentoring relationship is one of the key differences between mentors, counsellors and coaches, and perhaps goes some way to explain the *Oxford English Dictionary*'s definition as a 'friend'. Clutterbuck and Megginson (1999) also make the link between 'mentor' and 'friend', a term which is almost certainly deemed irrelevant or even inappropriate in a coaching relationship and would be viewed as unethical in counselling. That is not to say that a mentor has also to be a friend, but rather that the nature of the mentoring relationship is more akin to that of friendship – with easy and direct contact, short and often-unplanned meetings, and a relaxed sharing of stories and experiences. That said, the concept of goal-setting remains central (Grant, 2006), and it is through the mentoring relationship that goals are identified. For it is the experience of the mentor that is informing and enabling the mentee's learning and development. However, it is important to sound a note of caution here. In some contexts (schools for example) it may be that the mentor is employed by the organisation in a trusted adult role, the purpose of which is to enable pupils to remain 'on track'. This role can often be structured or, worse, authoritarian in nature, going against the principles of a mentoring relationship as introduced here (David *et al.*, 2013). Hassan is a student mentor in a university. He describes what this relationship involves.

Case study: Hassan (university mentor)

I think I'm what's called a 'peer mentor'. This means that I'm a student in my second year at uni and I'm mentoring Elise, a new student on the first year of her course. I used to be a 'learning buddy' when I was at school and I realise now that this was also all about mentoring, although I hadn't heard the word 'mentor' then. I'm studying geography and Elise is doing music, but it doesn't really matter that we're not actually doing the same course. I'm just there as someone to talk to when Elise needs me. For example, she's doing her first written assignment now, and she was getting in a right panic about plagiarism and referencing. She texted me and asked if we could meet up. We met in the student union and talked about her anxieties. I wasn't much help as I'm a bit hazy about referencing myself, but I was able to tell her to go to see the learning support staff in the library, who are great. She was a bit nervous about doing this, so I suggested that she come along with me, as I was going to the library anyway later that day, and I could introduce her. It's that sort of thing really. No big deal!

Hassan describes the role of peer mentor clearly. He says that it is 'no big deal' but, actually, mentors (like counsellors and coaches) need to have knowledge and understanding about effective one-to-one engagement with others and to work within the boundaries of a safe and trusting relationship. Mentoring focuses on:

- helping others to achieve their goals – usually in relation to education, health or employment, for example developing learning strategies, managing and giving up an addiction, or taking on a new employment role;
- building a professional but often relatively informal relationship – not a friendship exactly, but sharing some of the features of friendship in terms of arranging meetings as and when they are helpful, and not being authoritarian in nature (being in the relationship together, sharing experiences and so on);
- adhering to less rigorous boundaries – confidentiality and the keeping of client records are core elements of the work of a coach and a counsellor. The mentor will also be aware of the confidential aspect of the mentoring relationship, but records are often not required to be completed after every intervention. Like a coach, a mentor will know when it may be appropriate to refer their mentee for counselling, when issues are raised that fall outside the remit of the mentoring relationship;
- building a relationship of trust – the mentee will feel confident and comfortable to share their issues and concerns with their mentor.

- working towards positive change in learning and development – the aim of mentoring is to enable the mentee to feel more confident in relation to the issues for which they initially had a mentor. This may be related to education and learning, or training and development in the workplace, or help with health issues.

Take a moment to read Case Study 1 in Part II, which has been provided by a learning support assistant (mentor) working in a school. This offers a powerful example of the potential depth of a mentoring relationship.

Activity

Now that you have read my definitions of counselling, coaching and mentoring, go back to the earlier activity in this chapter, where I asked you to try to define each role. How far do your definitions agree with mine? What are the differences? Has engaging with the reading changed your view in any way?

Counselling, coaching and mentoring – shared features and distinctions

So far, we have examined each activity (counselling, coaching and mentoring) individually. Clearly there are differences, to some extent, in each approach. But we have seen that there are similarities too. Table 1.1 aims to set out the shared features and broad distinctions in counselling, coaching and mentoring roles.

It is clear that the shared features focus on the effective building of the relationship between the counsellor, coach or mentor and their client. In each case, the relationship requires the 'helper' to demonstrate empathy, to be genuine and real, and to accept their clients unconditionally. Furthermore, each accesses a shared range of helping skills and techniques in order to enable their client to move towards positive change in their lives.

The distinctions are to do with two important elements: first, the nature of the issues presented and the depth to which they are explored; and, second, the differences in theoretical orientation, which are a dominant feature in counselling but less so in coaching and mentoring.

With the growth of the helping professions comes the emergence of new roles. Many people engaged in helping relationships would not necessarily identify as counsellors, coaches or mentors, but, we would argue, these people are often building relationships of trust with clients and working towards change. So, the shared features in the table opposite are present in many helping-relationship roles.

Table 1.1 Counselling, coaching and mentoring – shared features and distinctions

	Counselling	Coaching	Mentoring
Shared features	Building an open, confidential, safe and trusting relationship with clients. Using effective helping skills in order to engage with clients' issues. Using a range of helping skills to work towards positive change. Demonstrating a non-judgemental approach to clients. Being empathic and genuine in the relationship.	Building an open, confidential, safe and trusting relationship with clients. Using effective helping skills in order to engage with clients' issues. Using a range of helping skills to work towards positive change. Demonstrating a non-judgemental approach to clients. Being empathic and genuine in the relationship.	Building an open, confidential, safe and trusting relationship with clients. Using effective helping skills in order to engage with clients' issues. Using a range of helping skills to work towards positive change. Demonstrating a non-judgemental and non-authoritarian approach to clients. Being empathic and genuine in the relationship.
Distinctions	Dealing with emotional, psychological and behavioural disturbance. Exploring issues at a deep level, working from a particular theoretical orientation (person-centred, CBT, integrative and so on). Can be long-term work – more than six sessions. Counsellors should be accredited and registered and receive regular supervision as a requirement to practise.	Dealing with personal and professional issues, often related to career and life development. Exploring issues in a goal-focused, positive manner. Using strategies and techniques to work towards change. Often using a coaching model or structure in their work. Often short-term work – fewer than six sessions.	Dealing with issues related to learning, health, work development. Meetings are often irregular and unplanned. It is usually the responsibility of the mentee to seek help from the mentor when required. The mentor will draw on and share their own experiences and knowledge as a way to assist mentees to consider strategies for change.

> ## Activity
>
> Take a look at Case Studies 4, 5, 6, 8, 9, and 10 in Part II. None of these helping professionals are employed specifically as counsellors, coaches or mentors, but each identifies the importance of the relationships they build and the helping skills that they access in order to work towards change with their clients.

The following chapters will examine the notion of a helping relationship in more depth. And from now on, the book will focus on the *shared* elements of helping rather than the *distinctions* in roles and approaches. The terminology adopted will be that of 'helper' rather than counsellor, coach or mentor, apart from where examples of practice and specific case studies from these professions are used as illustrations.

Summary

This chapter began with defining the term 'helping professions' by establishing the key features of counselling, coaching and mentoring relationships and identifying the professional contexts in which these roles take place. The chapter ends by considering the shared elements of each discipline and identifying the differences and distinctions in approach. The reading suggested below will help to develop your knowledge and understanding of counselling, coaching and mentoring and the broader helping role.

> ## Further reading suggestions
>
> Claringbull, N. (2010) *What is Counselling and Psychotherapy?* Exeter: Learning Matters – Clearly written, this text engages the reader and offers a sound insight into what counselling is all about.
>
> van Nieuwerburgh, C. (2014) *An Introduction to Coaching Skills: A Practical Guide.* London: Sage – A very accessible read that clearly explores the key features of coaching practice.
>
> Garvey, B., Stokes, P. and Megginson, G. (2014) *Coaching and Mentoring: Theory and Practice* (2nd edn). London: Sage – Part I of this book provides a helpful introduction to both coaching and mentoring and their development.

2

A HELPING MODEL

COUNSELLING, COACHING AND MENTORING

Chapter objectives: Readers will have the opportunity to ...

- define an integrative approach to helping;
- describe the key features of the person-centred core conditions;
- reflect on the application of the core conditions in practice;
- identify the key features of goal-orientated approaches to helping.

Introduction

Where the Introduction to this book and Chapter 1 introduced, in general terms, the concept of the helping professions, helping relationships and helping interventions, this chapter goes further by identifying and beginning to explore a helping model that can be applied in a range of professional contexts: counselling, coaching and mentoring. Whilst it is true to say that these disciplines have each developed their own models, structures and frameworks for effective helping practice (and some of these will be introduced here), it is also helpful to note that these models often share key features. In this chapter, a single model will be explored in depth – an integrative helping model that is underpinned by the core conditions of person-centred practice, whilst working towards positive, goal-orientated outcomes. This integrative model can be applied effectively in a range of helping interventions with clients, whether in long-term counselling relationships, one-off coaching sessions, on-going mentoring relationships, or short-term therapeutic practice.

An integrative approach to helping

The English verb 'to integrate' derives from the Latin *integrare*, meaning to make whole or to renew. Integration therefore is the act or process of combining several parts into a whole, or completing something that is not yet complete, by adding new parts.

Thus the term 'integration' implies a 'joining-together' or interweaving of two or more elements. For example we might talk about integration in relation to cultures and societies where two groups, each with their own set of values, beliefs, customs and norms, join together and, over time, develop into a single new group with its own unique identity, drawing on and underpinned by what has gone before. Often integration is an evolving concept and this is certainly true in the context of the helping professions.

The word 'integration' developed in the counselling profession in the latter half of the 20th century, and currently many counsellors and counsellor-training programmes describe their counselling orientation as integrative. Although an integrative approach is used in counselling, coaching and mentoring contexts and underpins a range of helping interventions, it is the counselling profession from which most theoretical models of practice – integration included – originated. So what follows offers a brief insight into the emergence of integration as a concept in counselling, before the approach was adopted more widely in coaching and mentoring contexts.

Prior to the development and growth of integration, counsellors would choose to train in a single therapeutic approach, whereby they would identify themselves with a specific psychological or philosophical perspective, for example: psychoanalytical (focusing on the subconscious and unresolved issues from the past); cognitive behavioural (examining the impact of negative or irrational thoughts on behaviour, and working to minimise these thoughts and change unwanted behaviours); or humanistic or person-centred counselling approaches (concerned with exploring feelings in the 'here and now'). Counselling students would learn about and adopt the underlying philosophy of their chosen approach and develop an accompanying set of skills and techniques. By so doing they would identify themselves as, for example, psychoanalytic, cognitive behavioural or person-centred counsellors. In other words, these counsellors could be described as *purist* in their approach.

Integration offers an alternative perspective to a purist approach. Reid and Westergaard explain: 'in brief, integrative counsellors draw from and integrate a range of theoretical perspectives in their counselling practice' (2011: 24). It is important to be clear that integration should not imply a 'pick-and-mix' approach to helping, whereby the helper selects on a whim a particular theoretical orientation, and skills and strategies to use with a client, dependent on whatever approach they feel like working with on that particular day. This would be unhelpful at best and potentially harmful, as counselling approaches and techniques often differ significantly in their underpinning philosophical and psychological beliefs and practice, making integration impossible. Rather, integration focuses on providing counsellors – or helpers – with a sound understanding of a number of key approaches, skills and techniques, and suggests a model which enables them to integrate these approaches, skills and techniques as appropriate, based on an accurate assessment of the needs of each client. Hollanders explains that 'integration covers a wide range of perspectives, making it impossible to present a unified set of theoretical assumptions in a way that may be possible for purist approaches' (2014: 522). McLeod clarifies in simple terms that 'the counsellor brings together elements from different theories and models into a new theory or model' (1998: 208). Worsley (2007) sets out his understanding of integration in more applied terms by explaining that he draws on and integrates any knowledge that helps him to understand the client, the process of therapy, and himself as the counsellor.

In spite of the rapid increase in the number of integrative counselling-training courses and the rise in practising counsellors who describe their orientation as integrative, integration in counselling has its critics. Eysenck (1970) proposed that integration would lead to what he describes as a mishmash of theories, procedures, therapies and other therapeutic activities which have no thought-through rationale and cannot be appraised, tested or evaluated reliably. Szasz (1974) concurred, suggesting that therapists who claim to work flexibly, basing their therapeutic approach on the needs of their clients, will only do so by assuming a variety of roles. He outlines these roles as magician, friend, physician and analyst, and argues that this lack of clarity and sense of purpose is likely to be unhelpful.

Whilst being mindful of these criticisms, it is also important to note that clients themselves, in helping relationships, are often unaware of the theoretical and technical orientation of the counsellor. And research has shown that it is the quality of the therapeutic relationship which clients value most and from which they often draw the support they need (Green, 2010; Hanley, 2012; Lynass et al., 2012). This therapeutic relationship, or alliance, is something that should be present in every helping intervention, regardless of the orientation of the counsellor.

Reflection point

Take a moment to reflect on your initial response to the concept of integration in helping relationships. How far do you, like many helpers, believe that it might be helpful to use a range of key skills and techniques in helping relationships in order to work towards positive change with clients? Alternatively, to what extent do you, like the critics of integration, believe that integrating different helping theories, skills and strategies might lead to a patchwork approach that may have the potential to be damaging?

You will of course have your own views, and what is offered in this book will help to inform those views. But it is important to be aware that what is provided here is an introduction to an integrative approach and model, which we believe can be effective across a range of helping contexts: counselling, coaching and mentoring. In the testimony below, Nadine, an integrative counsellor, explains what practising integratively means to her.

Case study: Nadine (counsellor)

I work as a school counsellor and I chose to train with an integrative approach. I'd had counselling myself, some years ago, and I remember that my counsellor told me on our first session together that she worked in an integrative way. I didn't know what this meant at the time, but she explained that she had an understanding of a range of different skills and techniques and that she would select the most appropriate way to work with me, once she had a clearer sense of who I was and what I wanted from counselling. I remember feeling comforted at the time that she was focusing on my needs and what would suit me best, rather than making me fit into what might feel like a limited or inappropriate approach for my needs at the time. So ... that's why, when the time came, I chose to train as an integrative counsellor. And this approach seems to work really well with the young people I see in school now. Sometimes a young person will want to focus on changing the way they think and behave, so I am mindful of goal-orientated approaches and techniques; sometimes they will want to come up with solutions to a specific problem, and then I find that solution-focused techniques work really well. At other times, a young person may just need me to sit and listen to their pain, and of course the core conditions of person-centred practice are central to the way I work and enable me to do this. That said, I have to ensure that my assessment of my clients is accurate and that my approach is flexible. It may be that the young person who comes to counselling initially because they just want someone to listen, over time, finds that they want to start working towards some kind of positive change in their lives. The integrative approach allows me the flexibility to engage with more goal-orientated practice in cases like this. It works for me and, much more importantly, it seems to work for my clients.

The core conditions of helping relationships

Later in this chapter an integrative model for helping will be introduced. As explained earlier, this model, like most integrative models, is underpinned by what are termed the 'core conditions' of a person-centred approach. The person-centred approach, proposed by Carl Rogers (1951) suggests that individual human beings are best placed to make decisions about their lives. Rogers believed that every one of us is the 'expert' in our own life and it is not the role of the helper, therefore, to provide answers and solutions to their clients' issues, but rather to enable their clients to identify the solutions that will work best for them. This can be a challenge for helpers. By their very nature counsellors, coaches and mentors are likely to be people who have chosen this work because they want to help to make things 'better' for others. Rogers would argue that the only person who has the capacity and resources to make things better in a meaningful way is the client themselves. By adhering to three core conditions, Rogers suggests that helpers can enable positive change to take place, and that clients can be supported to access their personal resources in order to reflect on their lives, make informed decisions, and take appropriate action where necessary. It is therefore important that the core conditions are introduced and explored here, as adherence to these conditions forms the bedrock of helping relationships and is central to an integrative model of practice. Reid and Westergaard, writing about integrative counselling with young people, explain:

> At the heart of integrative counselling practice, regardless of the different theoretical models and techniques that might be applied, lies the counsellor's adherence to the core conditions of a person-centred approach (Rogers and Stevens, 1967). The application of these core conditions coupled with the belief that young people have within themselves the resources and capacity for change (although these may be deeply buried and rarely glimpsed in some cases) should, over time, lead to the establishment of a trusting relationship: a therapeutic alliance. (2011: 40)

There are six conditions, introduced by Rogers as being central to effective helping practice. Mearns and Thorne (2013) detail the features of each. In summary, these conditions require that:

- there are two people – a helper and a client – who are in psychological and emotional contact;
- the client should be experiencing (to some degree) emotional, psychological or behavioural issues or difficulties;
- the helper should be willing to engage with the client, should be committed to them, and must build a relationship of trust in order to support them and enable them to find a way forward;
- the helper should be empathic, engaging with and working hard at all times to understand and relate to the client's world, their life and their experiences;
- the helper should be congruent: real, genuine and open in the relationship whilst being self-aware and reflexive – mindful of their own feelings and responses;
- the helper should demonstrate unconditional positive regard: mindful not to let preconceptions or judgements inhibit their ability to engage with clients; they should respect their client's right to hold their beliefs and live by their values, and should work hard to ensure a non-judgemental approach in the counselling relationship.

It is the latter three of the six conditions listed above that are commonly referred to as the core conditions. And it is these that firmly underpin an integrative approach to helping and are therefore worthy of deeper exploration.

Empathy

It is important to be aware of the distinction between empathy and sympathy in the helping context. An empathic response to someone who has had a recent painful bereavement might be: 'I can sense how tough life feels for you right now.' A sympathetic response in the same situation might sound something like: 'Oh, you poor thing, I'm so sorry for you. I know just how you're feeling, but you'll feel better soon, I promise.' Sympathy has its place, but it is the demonstration of empathy with which a professional helping relationship is concerned. Helpers are never in a position to tell their clients that they know just how they are feeling, or to make promises that they will feel better soon. We cannot make these kinds of assurance to our clients, and neither can we possibly know exactly how another human being – with a unique set of experiences, emotions, physical make-up, values, sociocultural background, sexuality, religious beliefs, faith and so on – might feel and react in any given situation.

One person's response to an experience will be very different to another's. In fact each person's response will be totally unique, as it will be informed by the factors set out above, which are individual and not shared. McLeod explains that 'it is important to stay within the "frame of reference" of the client, to "walk in their shoes", to "see the world the way they see it", and not to respond on the basis of your own projections, experiences or to offer advice' (2004: 53). Mearns and Thorne make the point that empathy is not a 'skill' that is adopted and used intermittently. Rather it is a way of being, where the counsellor 'lays aside her own way of experiencing and perceiving reality, preferring to sense and respond to the experiences and perceptions of her client' (2013: 55).

Activity

What might be an empathic response to the client in the following scenarios?

1. A client tells you that she is unhappy at work, as she keeps getting 'passed over' for promotion.
2. A client is upset because he has slapped his child twice in the last week.
3. A client is delighted because over the past week she has been able to limit her alcohol intake, from a bottle of wine every night to two glasses.
4. A client is ashamed that he has copied another student's coursework, changed words 'here and there' and tried to pass it off as his own.
5. A woman tells you that she has done a 'terrible thing' and been unfaithful to her husband.

In each of the cases above, an empathic response would come from a congruent and non-judgemental perspective, reflecting the clients' own responses to the way they are feeling, rather than your own thoughts and feelings about what has taken place. Mearns and Thorne (2013) suggest four levels of empathy: level 0 demonstrates no understanding of the feelings that the client is expressing; level 1 demonstrates a partial understanding; level 2 demonstrates an accurate understanding; and level 3 goes further by demonstrating an accurate understanding of what is expressed *and* identifying underlying or unspoken emotions.

In summary, empathy means:

- working to understand thoughts, feelings, actions and consequences from your client's frame of reference;
- communicating this understanding accurately to clients;

- 'containing' or 'holding' clients' challenging and painful emotional responses;
- not rushing to 'make better' or 'fix' things that are challenging for clients;
- not offering sympathy ('Oh, you poor old thing!') to clients.

The skills required to communicate an empathic response to clients will be examined later in this book. For now, it is important to be aware of the concept of empathy and be mindful of its significance in the helping process. Each of the case studies that make up Part II of this book demonstrate clearly how practitioners in a range of helping contexts work hard to ensure that they adhere to the core condition of empathy in their work with clients. It might be useful to select three or four of the case studies and identify the core condition of empathy in each.

Congruence

Where empathy is a relatively straightforward concept to understand (but not always to adhere to), congruence can be a little more problematic. Mearns and Thorne explain that 'congruence is the state of being of the counsellor when her outward responses to her client consistently match her inner experiencing of her client' (2013: 100). Put simply, this means that the helper who demonstrates a congruent response is 'real' in the relationship, authentic, genuine and fully aware of their own thoughts, feelings and responses to their client. Rogers (1961) concurs and suggests that congruence is all about making sure that thoughts, feelings and responses are consistent and are expressed as such by the helper.

Being congruent requires great reflexivity and high levels of self-awareness on the part of the helper. Whilst engaging with clients, helpers are consistently asking themselves important questions:

- 'Why do I feel like this with this client?'
- 'Is my emotional response to this client about their experience, or about something in my life that has been triggered?'
- 'Why am I finding it hard to empathise with this client?'
- 'Why do I want to "parent" this client?'
- 'Why do I want this client to go away?'
- 'Why do I feel so bored when I'm with this client?'

A congruent response does not necessarily mean saying what you feel, but rather reflecting on your own emotional response and sharing your feelings if, and when, you decide it would be appropriate and helpful for your client. Johnny, a life-coach, describes a piece of work with a client where congruence was a challenge.

Case study: Johnny (life-coach)

I'd been seeing Sylvia over a period of a few months. I warmed to her and thought we were working really well together. She explained that she'd reached what she described as a 'crossroads' in her life and couldn't decide whether focusing on furthering her career or starting a family should be her priority. She was determined to give up work to care for her child, so she knew that, in the short term at least, she'd be sacrificing her career. I began to become aware that I had strong feelings about what particular course of action Sylvia should take. This is unusual as I know it's not my place to 'suggest' or 'recommend' a particular route, but rather to help my clients to weigh up the pros and cons of their options and reach their own conclusions. I became conscious of a strong impulse to suggest to Sylvia that she focus on her career – or at least to continue working even if she does decide to start a family – because she had a fantastic job that could potentially lead on to something very exciting. If I had been congruent, without also being reflexive, I might have said something like 'My feeling is that maybe another opportunity like this one won't come along again, and you'd be wise to stick with it a little longer. Perhaps you could consider continuing to work, even part time, once the baby is born?'

I shared my concerns with my supervisor about how helpful (or not) my congruent response might be. She helped me to reflect on where my feelings were coming from, and I realised that, actually, I was reliving painful memories from my own past when my mother consistently told me, as a young child, that she had 'wasted' her life on bringing me up – in other words, that this had little to do with my client at all. Once I had recognised this, I was able to resume work with Sylvia, and challenge her to consider all the options open to her and their consequences, in detail. She was happy with the decision she reached and in our last session together she laughed as she said, 'Thank you for helping me to think things through so clearly, without telling me what you think I should do. I've got enough people doing that already! I just needed to think about what was right for me.'

Johnny was self-aware enough to know that his feelings needed careful reflection before he was able to decide how to respond to his client, in her best interest. He was able to discuss this in supervision and to realise that his own life experiences were in danger of influencing his work with Sylvia. Of course, there will be plenty of times when it would be helpful to respond directly in the helping relationship for the benefit of the client. For example, if a client presents as particularly aggressive and antagonistic, you may want to say, 'Sometimes when I'm with you I find myself feeling anxious or even frightened. I wonder how it feels to hear me say that?'

Activity

How would you manage your feelings and responses in the following scenarios whilst remaining congruent?

- You are frustrated by a client with whom you have been working over a long period of time, who seems unable to act on any decisions she makes.
- You think that your client is attracted to you, and you are aware that you are feeling attracted to them too.
- You feel angry with the wife when working with a couple. She consistently puts her husband down and only ever makes negative comments about him.
- You are working with a young man who expresses openly racist views.

There are no right or wrong responses to the scenarios outlined above. What is important is to be aware of – and congruent – about what we are feeling, and analyse whether or not it would assist the client to gain greater insight about their own situation if we shared our thoughts and feelings with them. Like Johnny in the case study above, it is imperative that helpers develop heightened self-awareness and use their own supervision effectively to reflect on appropriate ways of responding to clients, keeping their clients' best interests at heart at all times – rather than simply finding ways of relieving their own frustration in the helping relationship. Case Study 3 in Part II offers a helpful illustration of congruence and is worth a read now.

Unconditional positive regard

The core condition of unconditional positive regard, like congruence, is complex and is often challenging for helpers to understand fully and adhere to. Mearns and Thorne (2013) suggest that helpers who demonstrate unconditional positive regard value the humanity of their clients and will not be deterred from this valuing by whatever the client says or does. The counsellor will consistently accept and demonstrate an attitude of warmth towards their client. Put simply, demonstrating unconditional positive regard (UPR) means accepting every client's right to their own beliefs, values, behaviours and experiences. This can be a challenge for helpers when they come across beliefs, values, behaviours and experiences that are very different to their own – and may even be abhorrent to them. Those who are in the early stages of their training for work in the helping professions often struggle with the concept of UPR. But it is important to stress that demonstrating UPR does not mean having to like or agree with our clients – but rather to respect their right to hold their beliefs and to value each client as a unique fellow human being. We cannot be in a position to judge others, as we have not lived their lives or experienced the settings in which these beliefs and behaviours have developed. Prever (2010) reminds us how Wilkins emphasises the need to engage with 'the person behind the "repulsive" or "repugnant" behaviour or attitude' (2001: 42).

Sometimes, this core condition is defined as a 'non-judgemental' attitude. This is accurate, to a point, but it is important to be aware that it is part of the human condition to make judgements about others – indeed this can be an effective survival mechanism. So helpers must be congruent and self-aware enough to recognise the judgements they are making and work hard to ensure that these are managed effectively and do not interfere in the context of their helping relationships.

Demonstrating UPR can be challenging for the reasons stated above. Every helper at some point will be faced with a client who presents experiences, views and beliefs that the helper struggles to understand, or finds unacceptable. However, Rogers was clear that over time, if the helper is able to accept their client unconditionally, then a relationship of trust will be built, the client will begin to know and accept themselves without feeling judged, and positive change is likely to take place as a result.

Activity

On a scale of 1–10 (with 1 being 'Very difficult' and 10 being 'Not difficult at all'), how challenging might you find it to demonstrate UPR in the following situations?

- A young client tells you that she supplies drugs to pupils in her younger sister's school.
- A male client explains that he has a history of domestic violence against women.
- A female survivor of child abuse discloses that she is also an abuser.
- A client asks you to pray with him.
- A client tells you that they are in love with you.
- A middle-aged daughter confides that she has thought about ending the life of her elderly, invalided parent.
- A young person confides that they have always felt trapped in the wrong gender and they want to change.
- A client consistently repeats unhelpful behaviours that you have devoted significant time in working to eliminate in the helping relationship.

As is the case with other activities in this chapter, there are no right or wrong answers. What is important here is that you are able to recognise the possible limitations on your own UPR. This does not mean that you should not engage in helping relationships with the clients in the list above where you scored 1, 2 or 3, but rather that you develop an awareness of your feelings and make a decision about how you can engage effectively in each case. If we are congruent, we will reflect on the times that we may wish to share our concerns or discomfort, but we must be mindful about how we can do this in a way that is beneficial for clients. With the help of supervision, in practice, you will be able to identify clients with whom you may feel unable to engage because, for whatever reason, your ability to demonstrate UPR may be compromised. You might also reflect on strategies for sharing your concerns with clients in a positive way, whilst keeping the relationship of trust intact. Case Study 4 in Part II is a good example of how the NHS community drugs and alcohol worker demonstrates UPR with her client.

To summarise, the core conditions proposed by Rogers remain central to helping practice. Counsellors, coaches and mentors learn about and adhere to these conditions in their work with clients in order to build and maintain relationships of trust, where clients feel able to be themselves, not be judged, to reach decisions about their lives, and to take action for positive change. These conditions, initially emerging from person-centred practice, also form the basis of an integrative approach to helping and will underpin any integrative helping model.

An integrative model for helping

The concept of a 'model' in the helping context is focused on offering an effective, practical structure for one-to-one interventions with clients. So when we say an 'integrative helping model', we are seeking to describe the process or mechanics of helping – what needs to happen in the helping relationship for it to be effective. A model provides helpers with a structure, a framework, a way of engaging with clients which enables them to remain focused and purposeful in their work. An integrative model offers the opportunity for helpers to integrate a range of skills, techniques and concepts as appropriate, whilst adhering to the core conditions discussed earlier. Without a model within which to work, helpers risk their helping practice becoming directionless and lacking in focus and purpose. A model is what is needed in order to set a 'helping' intervention apart from a 'cosy chat'.

There are a range of helping models in counselling, coaching and mentoring, some of which are outlined briefly below.

Systematic, integrative relational model – counselling
(Murphy and Gilbert, 2000)

Focuses on the relationship between counsellor and client and identifies six key stages of the relationship:

1. 'Is it possible for us to work together?'
2. The first meeting and assessment: 'How will we work together? What do we want to work on?'
3. Establishing trust: the working alliance – a deeper exploration of clients' issues.
4. Moving through: the process of exploration and change of potentially negative internal dialogues.
5. Experimenting in the present and living new choices: supporting clients in putting their new self-knowledge into practice.
6. Saying goodbye: ending the relationship appropriately.

An integrative model – counselling (Geldard and Geldard, 2005)

Focuses on seven key stages of the helping process:

1. Preparation – what help is the client seeking?
2. Joining – the beginnings of a trusting relationship.
3. Active listening – the client tells their story.
4. Emphasis on emotions – client is enabled to explore and release their emotions.
5. Emphasis on thoughts – clarifying the problem, identifying any negative/unhelpful thought patterns, restructuring the thoughts.
6. Emphasis on behaviour – considering the options, committing to change.
7. Closure – the relationship ends.

Integrative counselling skills model – counselling
(Culley and Bond, 2011)

Focuses on skills used at each of three stages in the counselling process:

- Beginning – establish the relationship, identify the presenting issue, assess the client's need, agree a contract for working together.
- Middle – reassess problems, maintain a therapeutic relationship, challenge.
- End – decide on appropriate change, implement change, end the working relationship.

The GROW model – coaching (Whitmore, 1992)

Concerned with the stages of goal setting and action planning:

- Goal – 'What would I like to achieve?'
- Reality – 'What is the current situation in relation to my goal?'
- Options – 'What options are there for me which will help me to achieve my goal?'
- Will – 'What action will I take as a result of the helping process?'

A model for mentoring – mentoring (Alred et al., 1998)

Operates on a three-stage basis:

1. Exploration – to explore issues which are identified by the mentored individual.
2. New understanding – gaining new perspectives and ideas.
3. Action planning – considering possible action steps and committing to them.

Mentoring process model – mentoring (Cooper and Wheeler, 2010)

A five-phase process model:

- Purpose – why is mentoring appropriate in this case?.
- Engagement – building a relationship between mentor and mentee.
- Planning – identifying what needs to be worked on and identifying goals.
- Emergence – putting actions into practice in order to achieve goals.
- Completion – reflecting on and ending the relationship.

The single interactional model – a range of 'one-off' helping contexts (Reid and Fielding, 2007)

A three-stage model used in single helping contexts (for example career guidance):

1. Negotiating the contract and agreeing an agenda.
2. Developing issues and identifying goals.
3. Designing, planning and implementing action.

The skilled helper model – a range of helping contexts (Egan, 2007)

A three-stage helping model used in a range of counselling and helping contexts:

1. Current scenario – 'Where am I now?'
2. Preferred scenario – 'Where do I want to be?'
3. Strategy – getting there: 'How am I going to get to where I want to be?'

There is insufficient opportunity here to explore each model in depth. What is striking, however, are the similarities between each, in that most suggest 'stages' through which the helping process develops, in order that clients are enabled to remain focused and to achieve realistic goals. The model we will focus on in more depth here is Egan's skilled helper model, which is widely recognised and used in a range of helping contexts, including counselling, coaching and mentoring. The model offers a clear framework within which helpers can build their relationships with clients and work in a meaningful and goal-orientated way. Reid and Westergaard explain:

> The purpose of the model was not to provide a new orientation to practise or an alternative psychological or philosophical perspective, but rather to offer a practical, easily accessible framework for counsellors to work within. Egan's model does not align itself with a particular counselling orientation (although Egan stresses the importance of adhering to person-centred core conditions in practice), neither does it exclude any complementary approach to counselling. (2011: 30)

Egan's three-stage helping model

As explained above, Egan's model is built upon three stages. This is not to suggest that the model is inflexible or formulaic, but rather that it offers helpers a clear sense of direction without being prescriptive. Reid and Westergaard (2011: 30–31) describe each stage of the model in some detail:

Stage 1: 'What's going on?'

*   Establishing a relationship of openness and trust.
*   Enabling the client to 'tell their story'.
*   Establishing the nature, breadth and depth of the issues raised.
*   Agreeing the focus or agenda for counselling by exploring the presenting issues in some depth.
*   Sharing expectations about what can be achieved.

Stage 2: 'What solutions make sense for me?'

- Exploring issues in more depth.
- Focusing on feelings and behaviour.
- Challenging perceptions and reframing where appropriate.
- Considering and evaluating options for change.
- Identifying a 'preferred scenario'.
- Establishing possible barriers to change.
- Identifying strategies to overcome barriers to change.

Stage 3: 'How do I get what I need or want?'

- Identifying possible action steps.
- Evaluating the pros and cons of action.
- Planning specific SMART (specific, measurable, achievable, realistic, time-bound) action steps.
- Setting timescales for action.

It is helpful to note that it is likely to take time to work through each stage of the process. It may be that several meetings are needed for the client to 'tell their story' in Stage 1 and for a relationship of trust to develop. Likewise, clients may appear to have reached Stage 3 and begun to identify possible action steps when another, more significant issue emerges which requires deeper exploration. Where this is the case, the process will move back to Stage 1 or 2. The skills required by helpers to assist their clients to work through this model will be explored in detail later in the book (see Chapters 3 and 4). The processes of contracting, agenda setting, goal setting and action planning will also be explored (see Chapter 5). For now, it is important to be aware of the need to take a structured approach to helping that is both flexible and goal focused.

Activity

Identify which stage of the model each of the following helpers and clients has reached, and consider what needs to happen in order to move to the next stage.

1. Kirsty, a learning mentor, has met Luke on six occasions. He has explained to her that he is struggling with his learning because of 'things that are going on at home'. Kirsty has explained her role to Luke and they have built an effective relationship. Kirsty

wants to help Luke to think about how he can make changes to overcome his problems, but as yet, Luke has not divulged what the problems are.

2. Ahmed is a coach, employed in a large organisation. He has been working with Julia for five sessions. They have established that Julia is unhappy in her current job role; although she enjoys working for the company, she does not feel that there are sufficient opportunities there for progression.

3. Mark is an addiction counsellor. He has been working with Ben for over a year. Together they have discussed a range of strategies to manage Ben's drug addiction. Ben has put some of these strategies into practice, but with little success. Ben is feeling despondent as he seems unable to stick to the strategies that have been agreed on for more than a couple of months.

4. Anna is a school counsellor. She is working with Emily, who has been self-harming. They have met on four occasions and explored the reasons behind the self-harm. Together they have discussed some possible strategies and Emily feels ready to put these into practice.

The examples above demonstrate that the helping process is not always straightforward, and is rarely linear. Human beings are complex and our lives are often complicated and messy, and therefore the way in which helpers work with their clients requires flexibility. However, without a model to support this process, the work risks lacking in focus and can very quickly become disjointed and muddled with no clear structure and means for progression. Egan's model is recommended here, but any of the models identified earlier in the chapter are also worthy of further exploration. Most helpers – counsellors, coaches and mentors – go on to develop their own helping models for practice, based on the kind of staged approach suggested here.

Summary

This chapter set out to introduce an integrative model for helping. It began by defining the term 'integration' and described the development of the integrative approach in counselling practice. The core conditions of empathy, congruence and unconditional positive regard were introduced and explored. Finally, Egan's three-stage integrative helping model was defined. The reading outlined below will help to develop your understanding further, whilst the case studies in Part II will assist you to demonstrate the process of helping and the application of a helping model in context.

Further reading suggestions

Egan, G. (2007) *The Skilled Helper* (8th edn). Pacific Grove, CA: Brooks/ Cole – The seminal text which introduces Egan's skilled helper model.

Reid, H.L. and Westergaard, J. (2011) *Effective Counselling with Young People.* Exeter: Learning Matters – Chapter 3 of this accessible text explores an integrative approach to counselling with young people.

Mearns, D. and Thorne, B. (2013) *Person-Centred Counselling in Action* (4th edn). London: Sage – A comprehensive introduction to the core conditions of person-centred practice.

3

FOUNDATION SKILLS FOR EFFECTIVE HELPING

Chapter objectives: Readers will have the opportunity to …

- identify foundation counselling and helping skills;
- consider how these skills are used in the helping context;
- develop their own use of helping skills by engaging with the activities suggested through the chapter.

Introduction

So far, this book has placed an emphasis on the fact that effective helping – counselling, coaching and mentoring – is neither a cosy chat nor a mutually beneficial conversation nor a monologue. Rather it is a purposeful and goal-orientated intervention that provides opportunities for developing in-depth reflection and understanding on the part of clients, whilst they work towards positive change in their lives. In order to engage in a meaningful way with clients, helpers are required to develop knowledge and skills in two key areas. First, they need to understand and adopt a particular approach, or model, to their helping practice (see Chapter 2 for my ideas about what this helping model might look like). Second, they should develop a sophisticated skill-set which enables them to listen actively to their clients, explore thoughts, feelings and experiences with their clients, encourage reflection, enable challenge, and assist clients to identify goals and take action.

It is important, first, to be clear about what is meant by the term 'skill'. There can be confusion around the terminology relating to helping, where we refer to 'approaches', 'attitudes', 'techniques', 'strategies' and 'skills'. These terms are used frequently in the helping literature, often interchangeably. In order to ensure clarity, these different concepts are set out and defined below.

- *Approaches* – the theoretical orientation of the helper, for example person-centred approach, cognitive behavioural approach or integrative approach; and the model or structure that is adopted in helping interventions, for example Egan's three-stage model (see Chapter 2, which focuses on approaches).
- *Attitudes* – the way in which the helper is open to and responds to their client. The core conditions of empathy, congruence and unconditional positive regard are examples of attitudes that the helper will possess and demonstrate throughout their work (see Chapter 2 for an exploration of attitudes).
- *Techniques* – specific activities or interventions with which helpers encourage their clients to engage in order to work towards positive change. These might include goal-setting or action-planning techniques (see Chapter 5) or techniques which are related to a particular theoretical orientation or approach, for example: thought stopping, systematic desensitisation or visualisation, all of which are related to cognitive behavioural therapy (CBT).
- *Strategies* – again, these are likely to be linked to a particular approach or orientation. So in relation to cognitive behavioural therapy, strategies might include adopting a range of techniques (see above) to change irrational or negative thoughts. In the helping professions, the strategy adopted by a helper relates directly to what it is that the client wants to work on, for example: improving confidence, developing self-esteem, making sense of the past, and so on.
- *Skills* – the specific interventions that helpers make as part of every helping interaction. These would include the skill of active listening, helpful questioning, summarising, silence, challenge, reflecting back and others. The skills are what the helper actually uses – *does* and *says* – in sessions with clients. And it is the skills of helping with which this chapter is concerned.

The expression 'helping skills' implies a generic range of interpersonal and conversational skills which those of us who work in helping relationships will develop specifically for the helping context. This is true, to a great extent, but it is important to be aware that helping skills are highly specialised and are in fact 'counselling skills' which have been developed in the counselling profession. So, where you see reference made to 'helping skills', you will know that these are actually counselling skills and that they are the skills used by professionals working in a range of helping contexts – counselling, coaching and mentoring.

This chapter introduces the foundation skills of helping. It focuses on the four skills identified below:

- Active listening
- Helpful questioning
- Reflecting back
- Summarising

The chapter will define each skill, explore how it can be used to aid effective helping, and provide opportunities for you to practise and develop each skill to ensure greater effectiveness in your own helping practice with clients. Chapter 4 will develop this theme further by focusing on advanced helping skills. But let us ensure that the important foundation skills are in place first.

Active listening

The ability to attend and listen with empathy to clients is not straightforward but it is crucial in order to establish, develop and maintain an effective helping relationship. Geldard and Geldard point out that 'a counsellor is primarily a listener. By listening to what the client says, the counsellor is able to help them to sort through their confusion, identify their dilemmas, explore their options, and come away from the counselling session feeling that something useful has occurred' (2005: 40). But listening in the helping context is different to – and more complex than – listening in normal conversation.

Activity: Active listening – key features

Think for a moment about what is meant by active listening. What do you think are the key features of active listening and how might active listening in the helping context be different to engaging in conversations with family and friends?

Where listening in an everyday conversation is likely to involve interruptions, talking over each other, wanting to get our own point across regardless of others, making assumptions, second guessing and so on, active listening is quite different. It involves the helper immersing themselves totally in what their client is saying – listening closely to the words clients are selecting, their tone of voice, their demeanour, their facial expressions, their body language and, importantly, what they are choosing *not* to say. Reid and Westergaard explain that 'the skill of active listening is the ability to listen deeper than the words. It is about "listening" with all our senses' (2011: 47). Tariq, a patient support worker in a large hospital, highlights the importance of active listening in his work.

Case study: Tariq (patient support worker)

When I applied for this job, the application form specified 'good listening skills'. Having been in my post for over a year now, I absolutely know why it is so important to listen. Often I am dealing with people who are in distress, in pain, confused, or are frightened. They don't always express these emotions in the words they are using – in fact very few people actually say 'I am upset' or 'I am confused' or 'I am scared'. So I have to listen to the other clues, the signals, the signs – the non-verbal cues like avoiding eye contact, a tremor in the voice, or an aggressive response that actually masks fear or pain – to gain a real understanding of how these people are feeling. It's important for me not to make assumptions, but to listen deeply, quietly, without interruption, with my eyes as well as my ears, and to try to see or 'feel' the whole picture. Patients often tell me that they like how I always seem to have time to listen to them. They often say that they find themselves saying things to me that they don't say to anyone else. This isn't always easy as I don't have a lot of time to spend with each patient, so I have to make what little time I do have count. I feel privileged to be doing this work.

Tariq emphasises the importance of listening actively and accurately to clients. He talks about the need to pick up on what is being kept hidden and not being said. Our bodies provide give-away signs – often ones that we are unable to control – which, if read correctly, can offer real insight into our client's world.

Activity: Not listening – how does it feel?

Take it in turns to talk with a friend about what you did last weekend. Whilst you are talking, your partner should make every effort *not* to show they are listening. There should be no verbal responses, no questions, no eye contact, and no interest whatsoever expressed by the 'listener'. Now swap over! Take a few moments to share your feedback with your partner. How did it feel not to be listened to? How did it feel not to listen?

It is likely that this activity did not take long to complete. It is very difficult to 'keep going' when we are not being listened to. You may have experienced a range of emotions including, anger, frustration or even worthlessness whilst trying to talk to someone who was not listening to what you had to say. If this level of inattention is present in a helping relationship, the client is likely to come away from the experience feeling deflated at best, and potentially damaged – in fact the helping relationship is unlikely to exist at all where this is the case.

In summary, active listening means:

- Listening with all our senses – our eyes, as well as our ears and the sixth sense, that of 'feel' or intuition.
- Listening without interruption – in a helping interaction, a good 'rule of thumb' suggests that the helper does not talk for more than 20% of the time.
- Listening to what is *not* being said as well as what *is* being said – What are the feelings behind the words? What is our client's body language telling us?
- Being aware of cultural factors – it is important not to make assumptions about non-verbal responses. For example we cannot assume that a client who does not engage in eye contact with us is shy or withdrawn. It may be that the cultural background of the client suggests that direct eye contact with a professional is disrespectful. As a helper, it is your responsibility to make yourself aware of the cultural norms of the client group with whom you work (see Chapter 8).

We demonstrate that we are listening through appropriate use of:

- *Eye contact* – maintain steady eye contact, but do not stare fixedly. You will know from the previous activity that if eye contact is not there, the impact on the client can be devastating. Try to avoid anything that detracts from maintaining eye contact, for example copious note-taking.
- *Body posture* – keep an open body posture, avoid crossed arms (which can be perceived as defensive), and sit at a comfortable distance from your client. Minimise any physical barriers between you and the client, for example desks and computers.
- *Facial expressions* – be sensitive to your client's expressions and respond accordingly. It would not be appropriate to display a huge grin if your client is in tears and talking about something distressing.

- *Verbal and non-verbal responses* – whilst helpers are reading their clients' verbal and non-verbal responses, we should also be aware that clients are picking up on the ways in which we respond to them in the helping context. For example, the flicker of a frown from a helper, the barely audible sigh of frustration or disapproval, or the vigorous nodding in response to something the client has said with which we agree – these will each be received and responded to by the client. A warm and open expression is important in order to convey listening and acceptance of clients.

Culley and Bond (2011) suggest that helpers are listening to four separate (but connected) elements. These are:

- experiences – what clients experience as happening to them in their lives;
- behaviour – how clients act; what they do or say in different situations;
- feelings – what clients feel about their behaviour, experiences, thoughts and actions;
- thoughts – what clients understand about their own and others' behaviour; what beliefs they hold about themselves, others and events in their lives.

Being aware of these four elements can help to focus our listening, to ensure that we are helping clients to explore every aspect of themselves: their experiences, behaviour, feelings and thoughts. In an ideal world, helping will take place in an environment that is conducive to promoting active listening. A confidential space should be available which is comfortable, but without too many visual distractions (pictures and ornaments, for example). However, helpers will know that at times the environment in which they work does not, for a range of reasons, feel a safe and comfortable space for clients. And it is not only environmental factors that can get in the way of active listening.

Activity: Barriers to effective listening

Take a moment to think about and write down possible factors that might impact on your ability to listen actively whilst demonstrating unconditional positive regard to your client. If you are currently engaged in practice, think about the environment in which you work. Try to think, too, about other non-environmental barriers to listening.

I am sure that you were able to identify factors (apart from practical and environmental issues) that might hinder your ability to listen actively, with acceptance. I have listed my ideas below:

- Trying to think of a solution – this can be particularly tricky as most of us have chosen to work in the helping professions because we want to help! However, this does not mean telling clients what to do or generating solutions to their problems. If we are working in a truly person-centred way, we cannot expect to know what is best for our clients, as we are not living and experiencing their lives.
- Values – our own value system and beliefs may get in the way of listening to someone who doesn't share our views.
- Issues in our own lives – we may be preoccupied and less 'open' to others if we are experiencing issues and challenges in our own lives.
- Being nervous and formulating a reply whilst the client is still talking – this is common whilst helpers are inexperienced or in training. It can be difficult to focus on what is being said in the 'here and now' if we are busy trying to think of the next question to ask.
- Seeking confirmation to our hypothesis – again, inexperienced helpers may feel that they have 'diagnosed' their clients, and anything the client says which may support that diagnosis is listened to, whilst things that are said which do not support the diagnosis are ignored or rejected.
- Feeling frustrated – if clients find it hard to articulate clearly, and express their feelings in a way that is muddled, confused and difficult to grasp or understand.
- Making assumptions – concerning how our client may be feeling about and experiencing an issue in their life.
- Becoming defensive, or labelling ourselves inadequate – if our client disagrees with us.
- Feeling anxious and out of our depth – about the experiences, thoughts and feelings our client is sharing.

Active listening is a fundamental skill which forms the bedrock to all helping interventions – counselling, coaching or mentoring – and it is important never to underestimate the power of being listened to. All the case studies from real practice in Part II emphasise the need for excellent listening skills and demonstrate the importance of listening in practice. Case Study 3 illustrates how the telephone counsellor must ensure that her active listening is able to 'pick up' the nuances of what her clients are saying – particularly as she only has the sense of hearing to rely on. That said, helpers are more than listeners. They engage with their clients using a range of skills in order to enable their clients to reflect, understand and make changes as appropriate. Developing the skill of questioning, alongside effective listening, is equally important.

Helpful questioning

Let me begin this section on helpful questioning by posing a question for you to consider: What is the purpose of questioning in the context of a helping intervention? Take a moment to reflect on this and form your response.

You might have considered a number of reasons for asking clients questions, including finding out information, clarifying what the client is saying, and asking the client to probe more deeply, expand and tell you more. These responses are valid, but there is a more important reason for asking questions. Reid and Westergaard explain:

> The primary purpose of questioning is to invite clients to think in detail about their lives. It encourages reflection, analysis and evaluation, invites clients to 'think through' their ideas and feelings, and establishes the nature and depth of the issues which they are facing. (2011: 50)

The skill of helpful questioning is, first and foremost, about offering clients an opportunity to pause, think deeply, reflect and consider their response carefully. It is this in-depth exploration of experiences, thoughts, feelings and actions that is at the centre of any helping relationship. Clients should leave the intervention feeling that they have discovered something about themselves or illuminated an issue more clearly, thought about things in considerable depth, and even challenged their self-perceptions. It is often the questions posed by the helper that will facilitate this level of increased self-discovery and self-awareness.

It is important to be aware that there are different types of question – some more and some less helpful – that counsellors, coaches and mentors are able to access. These include:

- *Open questions* – require more than a yes/no response; for example, 'How did you feel when that happened?'
- *Hypothetical questions* – invite clients to think about a scenario that has not necessarily happened, to consider how they would respond. This type of questioning is often referred to as 'what if' questioning; for example, 'If she said that to you, what do you imagine you might say back?'
- *Closed questions* – demand a yes/no response; for example, 'Did you feel sad?'
- *Multiple questions* – where two or more questions are asked without a pause; for example, 'Tell me all about it. When did it happen? What did you say? How did you feel?'
- *Leading questions* – whereby the helper 'suggests' a response to clients within the question; for example, 'You probably wouldn't want to do that, would you?'

Activity: Helpful questions

Take a moment to scrutinise the questions in the list above. Which would you identify as helpful – and why? Are there any in the list that you would say are positively unhelpful?

Generally, closed, multiple and leading questions are best avoided in the helping context. Closed questions can sometimes be helpful if, for example, you are asking a client to clarify or be precise about a situation, experience, feeling or fact; but if overused, closed questions may start to resemble an interrogation. Multiple questions can be confusing for clients and it is likely that either the first or the last question will be the only one in the 'set' of three or four questions posed that is responded to. Leading questions are never helpful. They are laden with the helper's own judgements and it may be difficult for a client to disagree or dispute; they certainly do not aid reflection. Both open and hypothetical questions are practised consistently in helping interventions and are useful in enabling deep thought and reflection. The activity below helps to put the use of open and hypothetical questions into context.

Activity: Open and hypothetical questions in practice

Imagine that a client has spoken to you about his increased stress levels. How might asking the open questions identified below assist his exploration?

Open questions

- 'What is generally happening when you feel stressed?'
- 'How do your feelings of stress tend to start? What are the triggers?'
- 'At what times do you usually feel stressed?'
- 'Where are you when you feel stressed?'
- 'Who do you turn to for help you when you are feeling stressed?'
- 'Why do you think you feel stressed?' (Some experts in counselling, coaching and mentoring suggest that 'Why?' puts pressure on clients to justify themselves rather than to reflect. Perhaps use 'I wonder why ...?' instead.)

(Continued)

(Continued)

As a result of the exploration, the client reflects that it is in the workplace where he feels most stressed, due to increased pressure and a clash of personalities with his new boss.

So, how might the hypothetical questions listed below assist him to reflect further?

Hypothetical

- 'What do you imagine would happen if you talked to your boss openly about how you feel?'
- 'What do you imagine is the worst that could happen with regards to the pressure you are feeling at work?'
- 'How do you imagine you would approach a meeting with your boss if she asked to talk frankly to you about your performance at work?'
- 'If you were feeling confident in this situation at work, how would you be behaving differently?'

What the helper is aiming for here is to assist the client to reflect more deeply on his experience of stress and to identify how he might feel and respond in the hypothetically posed scenarios outlined above. This hypothetical exploration can lead to an examination of strategies and options that he may consider in order to begin to reduce his stress levels and improve his working relationship. That said, hypothetical questions naturally take clients into a future-orientated scenario, and a note of caution should be introduced here. If used prematurely, without sufficient exploration, there is a risk that clients are rushed into a solution or strategy stage before they have thought through their situation in depth.

The skill of questioning can be difficult to master. In our day-to-day conversations, we often find ourselves using closed questions with friends, family and colleagues, but generally these will be responded to as if they were open. For example:

Jenny: 'Did you enjoy your holiday, Chris?' (*Closed question*)
Chris: 'Oh I loved it! We did so much. When we arrived we...' (*Open response*)

In helping interventions, by contrast, and particularly when working with younger clients, a response to a closed question can serve to limit the interaction. For example:

Julian: 'Did you enjoy your recent work experience?' (*Closed question*)
Mehmet: 'No, not really.' (*Closed response*)

In the case study below, Janine, a trainee counsellor, talks about the importance of asking helpful questions.

Case study: Janine (trainee counsellor)

We haven't actually worked with clients yet, but we've been looking at questioning skills as part of our training and we've been practising these in role-play activities with each other. The first time we did a role play, we were told to try to avoid using closed questions. I thought that this would be easy, but I couldn't believe how tricky it was. I wasn't even aware how many closed questions I was asking until the person observing the role-player told me afterwards in feedback. I went through a period where I felt that all I could think of when doing a role play was asking the next open question and working out what that might be. This meant that I ended up not really listening to my 'clients'. My tutor suggested that I write a list of open questions to use and practise, and that I try putting the words 'I wonder' or 'how' in front of my closed questions to make them open. I found that both strategies really helped, and now my questions flow much more easily. If I do catch myself asking a closed question, I can follow it up by saying, 'Tell me a bit more about that.' Our tutor told us that we'd know when we asked a good question because our client is more likely to pause, reflect and take time to think about their response.

Janine makes the point that developing the important skill of helpful questioning is not as simple as it may appear. Although we ask questions every day in a range of contexts, we must be aware that the purpose of questioning in counselling, coaching and mentoring is specific and focused. Making use of open and hypothetical questions ensures that clients are given opportunities to reflect. That said, there may be times when an open or hypothetical question feels too challenging or 'big' for a client to engage with. It is important therefore to reflect that sometimes the question itself requires an explanation, for example: 'I'm going to ask you something now that might feel a little strange. The reason I'm going to ask this is because ...'

Janine's tutor is correct to say that good questions are likely to engender thoughtful responses. This can be seen in practice in Case Study 9 in Part II, which illustrates the powerful use of questioning skills when the care manager assistant discusses her work with her client.

Another skill that assists this process of reflection further is the skill known as 'reflecting back' or 'reflection'.

Reflection – reflecting back

The skill of reflection is closely allied to active listening. It requires the helper to reflect back – restate – a single word or short phrase in order that the client hears back what they have just said. This provides clients with the opportunity to reflect on the word they have used, consider the emphasis they have placed on the word, think deeply about why they have selected that word to express how they are feeling, and thus clarify their meaning further. Sometimes, particularly when emotions are running high, we select very powerful words to use. These words are not always a totally accurate expression of what we are feeling, but rather suggest a heightened or exaggerated response. It is important that clients are assisted to explore the strength of their feelings, and, by reflecting back key significant words, they are assisted to do this. The example below shows Susannah, a community health nurse, engaging with George, an elderly client whom she has been visiting for some months. The skill of reflection is highlighted throughout.

> ### Case study: Susannah (community health nurse) and George
>
> Susannah: 'How are you feeling today George?'
> George: 'Bloody terrible!'
> Susannah: 'You're feeling *terrible*?'
> George: 'Bloody terrible!'
> Susannah: 'And what does "*bloody terrible*" feel like?'
> George: 'Worse than I felt last week. A lot worse.'
> Susannah: '*Worse* than last week. In what way do you think you're feeling *worse*?'
> George: 'Well not worse really, not in my body, not physically. I've just felt so damn lonely this week.'
> Susannah: '*Lonely*. That sounds tough. And what has been different this week to make you feel so *lonely*?'

In the example above, Susannah does not try to 'jolly along' her client, but rather takes his words seriously and assists him to clarify his meaning by reflecting back the key, powerful and emotionally charged words he is using. Once he has expressed accurately how he is feeling and feels listened to, Susannah will go on to help George to think about strategies he might adopt to help him address his sense of loneliness. But use of more advanced skills is for the next chapter.

Care should be taken when reflecting back, to avoid 'parroting' every word your client is saying. This could be perceived by clients as unhelpful or even patronising if done consistently without thought for what the reflection is attempting to achieve. That said, the impact of hearing back our own words spoken by someone else, particularly when those words are laden with powerful emotions, should not be underestimated. Whereas listening and questioning are skills that are familiar to us, as we use them in everyday conversation – albeit in a different way to how we use them in helping interventions – reflecting back is not generally a conversational skill, but rather a skill that has been developed for use in counselling, coaching and mentoring contexts. For that reason, it may feel unfamiliar at first, or even clumsy when used in training and role-play activities.

In summary then, reflection means *restating* a single word or a short phrase used by a client in order to:

- check that you have heard and accurately understood your client's view;
- enable your client to reflect on what they have said: is that what they meant, or was there another, more complex meaning behind the word they selected?
- communicate empathy and unconditional positive regard to your client, thus building the helping relationship through developing rapport.

Mearns and Cooper suggest that 'invitations to the client to explore their experiences more deeply can take many forms. At the most basic level, it may simply involve reflecting back to clients a word or phrase they have used' (2005: 36). Culley and Bond concur with this analysis, explaining that 'restating involves repeating back to clients either single words or short phrases which they have used. It is an efficient way of prompting further discussion' (2011: 36). The skill of reflection is not dissimilar from the skills of summarising and paraphrasing, which we will explore next. However, although it shares some common features with these skills, reflection is an important skill in its own right which, when used effectively, can assist deeper understanding and promote greater insight for both client and helper.

Summarising and paraphrasing

The skills of summarising and paraphrasing are crucial to helping practice, but they are often under-used by helpers. Like reflection, summarising and paraphrasing are not natural conversational skills that are used in social settings when talking to friends, family and colleagues, for example. Rather they are counselling skills that need to be learned and practised in order to be used effectively in helping relationships with clients. Summarising and paraphrasing mean 'stating back' to clients the key points, issues and emotions they are expressing, but in the helper's own words. By so doing, the client has the opportunity to hear back their 'story' spoken by another person. This can be a powerful experience, as it demonstrates that it is the client and their words that are central; it helps clients to question and clarify – 'Is that what I said?', 'Is that what I meant?', 'I didn't realise that I actually felt like that', 'No, I don't think that's exactly right. It's more a case of ...'

Summarising and paraphrasing not only enable clients to gain greater understanding through reflection; they also demonstrate that the helper is actively listening, is engaged in the process, and is empathic, and therefore that the relationship of trust should continue to be built and strengthened. In the example below, Nathan, an occupational therapist, paraphrases and then summarises in his helping interventions with Gerry.

Case study: Nathan (occupational therapist)

Nathan: 'OK, Gerry, so you think that the most important thing for you right now is to have some help and support in preparing food and using the cooker. Can I just check that I've got that right?' (*Paraphrasing*)

Strategies are shared and discussed and, in the following week, at the start of the session:

Nathan: 'We talked last week about the kind of support that might be useful for you, Gerry. You've been feeling anxious that you haven't been feeding yourself properly because it's so difficult for you to prepare food and use the cooker. We came up with some suggestions, too, last time we met, for things you could try. How have you got on with those strategies? (*Summarising*)

The short example above demonstrates that summaries are essentially longer, more detailed paraphrases. The example also shows how Nathan is not simply summarising the *content* of what has been discussed, but is also reflecting back Gerry's *feelings* – anxiety, in this case. It might seem strange to start an intervention with a summary, as demonstrated above, but it is important to be aware that summaries are used throughout helping interactions (as are shorter paraphrases) and not saved until the end.

Culley and Bond (2011) recommend some ground rules when using summarising or paraphrasing. In brief, they suggest that helpers should:

- take a tentative approach and 'offer' their perception of what the client has said and their understanding of how the client is feeling;
- take care not to 'tell', 'inform', 'interpret', 'explain' or 'define' on behalf of the client;
- be respectful – avoiding making judgements or using sarcasm;
- use their own words to paraphrase or summarise; the aim is not to mimic or patronise clients, but to reach a shared understanding;
- ensure they listen to the depth of feeling in what clients are saying and match this in their response in order to demonstrate empathy;
- take care not to add to what has been said or attempt to embellish it;
- be real, genuine and congruent in their responses; it is important that helpers do not pretend to understand if they do not understand;
- be concise and direct, using language that is clear and unambiguous;
- take care to ensure that they keep the tone of the voice level.

This is a helpful checklist for summarising and paraphrasing. In a moment, there will be an opportunity to put all the skills in this chapter into practice in a role-play activity, but first let us attempt to revise what we know about the skills of summarising and paraphrasing.

Summarising and paraphrasing – how?

- Feed back the main points raised at key points during the interaction.
- Feed back the feelings and emotions underpinning the words.

Summarising and paraphrasing – why?

- To demonstrate listening.
- To enable clients to reflect on, understand more fully, and learn from what has been said.
- To clarify meaning.
- To help if the interaction is unfocused.
- To help if the interaction is 'stuck'.
- To demonstrate empathy.
- To encourage, develop and maintain a relationship of trust.
- To highlight key themes or tensions.
- To share, confirm and agree action points.

The activity outlined below offers the opportunity to put the skills of active listening, helpful questioning, reflection, paraphrasing and summarising into practice. Ideally, the activity involves three people – a helper, a client and an observer. The role of the observer is to watch the activity with a critical and analytical eye. Critical, in this context, does not mean 'negative' but rather a careful and focused observation, with clarity and awareness concerning what it is that they are looking out for. Where an observer is able to participate, it is important to be mindful of sensitivity around giving feedback. The guidelines below should be noted:

- In the first instance, before sharing feedback as the observer, ask the 'client' in the role play to share how they experienced the helping interaction.
- Again, before offering feedback, ask the helper to share their own 'observations' about what went well and what they felt needed development.
- Begin by sharing a positive observation – what did the helper do well?
- Assist the helper by inviting them to reflect on specific areas (skills, core conditions) that you feel may benefit from development; be tentative here, and avoid the urge to say 'If I were you I would have...'.
- End by summarising your observation of the interaction as a whole, in a positive and constructive way.

If you are unable to find someone to act as an observer, it might help to record your interaction using a mobile phone or other device. You can then listen back, reflect and undertake a deep analysis of the skills you used.

Activity: Using the foundation skills of helping

In threes, if possible, undertake a 15 minute helping intervention (a helper, a client and an observer). I have suggested some possible role-play scenarios to 'act out' below. Alternatively the person taking the role of 'client' may be happy to talk about a real issue in their own lives which they feel it might be useful to explore. If this is the case, the 'issue' should not be too emotionally challenging or overwhelming and the client should feel confident that they are keeping themselves safe by sharing.

The observer should attend to and feed back on the helper's use of:

- active listening;
- helpful questions;
- reflection;
- summarising and paraphrasing.

In addition, the observer should be mindful of the helper's ability to adhere to the core conditions.

Role play 1: You are a counsellor working in a school. A young person has been referred to you because they have told their tutor that they are unable to concentrate in school because they have discovered that their parents are separating.

Role play 2: You are a qualified nurse and a mentor to student nurses. Your mentee seeks you out as he is feeling overwhelmed by a combination of his workload and his studies.

Role play 3: You are a life-coach in private practice. A client makes an appointment because she has heard a rumour that her company is going to be making redundancies and she feels vulnerable in her current position.

This is a challenging activity and, of course, if you have recently embarked on your training in the helping professions, you will probably have found that there are a number of areas to develop. Even if you are an experienced practitioner, it can be helpful to take opportunities to reflect on practice, to examine your work closely, and to remind yourself of the importance of using skills mindfully and effectively. Seeking clients' agreement to record helping sessions can enable this learning and development process for practising counsellors, coaches and mentors.

Summary

This chapter set out to introduce the foundation skills of helping, used in a range of helping contexts. The point is made throughout the chapter that helping skills are counselling skills – some are social and conversational skills that are adapted for the helping context, whilst others have been developed for and are used specifically in helping interventions. Learning about these skills in a 'technical' way is important. Helpers should be very clear about what they are doing and why they are doing it and should be able to name, evaluate and analyse the skills they use in practice. That said, it is as important to develop a practical as well as an abstract knowledge of helping skills. Activities like role play can help this process enormously. For experienced practitioners, regular supervision provides the opportunity to put skills used in practice 'under the microscope' and have them scrutinised in order to ensure they remain finely honed and effective in supporting clients.

Further reading suggestions

Culley, S. and Bond, B. (2011) *Integrative Counselling Skills in Action* (3rd edn). London: Sage – A must-have text for anyone who is training or embarking on practice in the helping professions.

Geldard, K. and Geldard, G. (2005) *Practical Counselling Skills: An Integrative Approach*. London: Palgrave Macmillan – A book crammed with helpful suggestions for activities to develop counselling skills.

Nelson-Jones, R. (2012) *Basic Counselling Skills: A Helper's Manual* (3rd edn). London: Sage – A clearly written and engaging book that describes a range of counselling skills and techniques.

4

ADVANCED SKILLS FOR EFFECTIVE HELPING

Chapter objectives: Readers will have the opportunity to ...

- identify advanced counselling skills: information sharing, challenge, immediacy and silence;
- consider how these skills are used in the helping context;
- develop their own use of advanced counselling skills by engaging with the activities suggested through the chapter.

Introduction

The previous chapter began by defining the term 'skill'. Five key skills for effective helping were introduced: active listening, helpful questioning, reflection, summarising and paraphrasing. It is important that helpers familiarise themselves thoroughly with these foundation skills, and feel confident about using them, before moving on to develop and apply advanced helping skills in their counselling, coaching and mentoring practice. Applying the key skills explored in the previous chapter will enable helpers to build effective relationships with their clients. When these skills are used in conjunction with the core conditions of empathy, congruence and unconditional positive regard, a relationship of trust, often termed a 'therapeutic alliance', will be established. It is only once this alliance is in place that clients may feel empowered and confident enough to explore their thoughts, feelings and behaviours more deeply, and to move from stage 1 of Egan's integrative helping model (see Chapter 2) (where they are 'telling their story') to stages 2 and 3 of the process (where change is identified, planned and implemented).

This chapter continues to focus on the practical elements needed to ensure effective helping by identifying and exploring a range of advanced counselling and helping skills: information sharing, challenge, immediacy and silence. Each of these skills requires a clear understanding as to its purpose (when to use each skill and why) and its implementation (how to use the skill effectively). As in previous chapters, activities will be suggested throughout which provide an opportunity not only to learn about advanced helping skills, but also to practise, develop and apply them. Remember too that the case studies in Part II of this book offer an insight into how a range of helping skills are used in practice – and you will be signposted to these at key points in this chapter.

Before we explore the advanced skills in depth, let us begin with an activity which will enable you to reflect on what you believe 'advanced skills' might look and sound like and what their purpose is in the context of a helping intervention. This is a challenging activity that you can return to later in this chapter once your understanding is developed more fully. Do not worry if you are unsure. Just respond as fully as you can.

Activity: Advanced skills – features and purpose

Focus your thoughts on the four advanced counselling skills to be explored in this chapter: information sharing, challenge, immediacy and silence. For each skill, note down your thoughts about:

- The purpose of using this skill in a helping intervention – what might using this skill achieve for clients?
- The key features of the skill – what does it look/sound like?
- How effectively you believe you use this skill already – can you identify times now when you use the skill?
- What knowledge or practice you need to develop and how you will do this, in order to use the skill effectively.

As suggested earlier, at the end of the chapter I recommend that you return to this activity and see whether or not your perceptions have changed and how far your thoughts about each skill are confirmed. You may also have new ideas about how you can continue to develop these skills further.

We will begin our exploration of advanced helping skills by examining the skill of information sharing. This is perhaps the most contentious of the counselling skills. It may appear, at first sight, to go against the principle of adopting a person-centred approach to working with clients, as there is a risk that the helper could be perceived to take on the role of 'expert' in the relationship. What follows will explain how and why the skill of information sharing is appropriate in helping relationships, and will also demonstrate how, if done well, this skill can enhance the client's understanding of the options available to them and assist their decision making.

Information sharing

Reid and Fielding explain clearly the importance of the skill of information sharing when engaging in helping relationships with young people. They emphasise the significance of the terminology used here – information *sharing*, not information *giving*. They suggest that '"sharing" means a two-way process where both parties contribute' (2007: 77). The skill of information sharing is equally important in a range of helping relationships, with adult clients as well as with young people.

The important question to consider here is why we may be required to share information as part of the helping process. The answer to this lies in the fact that many people seek help when they are faced with difficult decisions in their lives. Often they feel confused about what options may be available to them and need help in thinking these options through in an objective and rational way. In the testimony below, Abdul, the career coach, explains when and how he shares information with clients.

Case study: Abdul (career coach)

My clients generally come to me because they are looking for some kind of career change. They may have been working in a job for some time and have decided that they'd like the challenge of a change of direction. Or maybe they feel that they have never actually found the job that is quite right for them. Anyway, whatever the reason, they often need information to help them to plan ahead. This could be information about different courses or training programmes, information about the labour market and job opportunities, or simply information about other career options. I have to be careful not to assume that my clients know nothing! I've made this mistake in the past and found myself bombarding clients with information that they already have. I stop when I see their eyes glazing over! I need to remind myself sometimes that my clients are not empty vessels waiting to be filled with my great knowledge!

Abdul makes the point that clients often need information in order to help them to find the option that is right for them and make realistic decisions and achievable plans for the future. He also sounds a note of caution in his testimony – reminding us that there is the risk that the dynamic between helper and counsellor, or coach/mentor and client, becomes one of 'expert–novice', 'healer–patient' or 'teacher–pupil'. The danger in this shift in relationship is that the core conditions of a person-centred approach may be compromised. The client, rather than taking ownership for their decision making, may look to the helper to 'solve', 'heal' or 'answer' the issue they are working through. This may ultimately lead to a disabling or even infantilising relationship between client and helper. This is not to say that helpers must not, on any account, share information with their clients, but rather they should be clear about why they are doing so and be mindful to ensure that, at all times, the client is an active and engaged participant in the sharing process.

Culley and Bond (2011) talk about 'providing information' and explain that using information can be helpful in a number of ways. Not only does appropriate information assist with the decision-making process, but also it can illuminate, reframe or normalise an issue or feeling that a client may be experiencing. In the example below, Jeff, a youth justice worker, demonstrates his use of information sharing in this intervention with his client, Suzy.

Case study: Jeff (youth justice worker) and Suzy – sharing information

Suzy: 'I just feel crap about what I did. I think about it all the time. Why did I do it? It was so stupid. There's no way that I'm ever going to be offered a job now, is there?'

Jeff: 'You're feeling fed up, Suzy, because you're taking responsibility for your actions and you're unhappy about what you did, and that is understandable. This is often how people in your situation feel at this particular time, as they're reflecting on the past and thinking ahead to their future.' (*Sharing information to acknowledge and normalise Suzy's feelings*)

Suzy: 'Really? And what happens to those people? Do they ever get jobs? Or do they end up like me, out of work and living a shit life?'

Jeff: 'Well, I'm sure that you know it would be an offence for any employer to refuse to offer you a job because of your conviction, Suzy? (*Information sharing to enable Suzy to understand the technicalities of disclosing her conviction*) Other young people I've worked with who

> have similar convictions are now working in jobs that they are very happy in, and they don't feel that their conviction has held them back. But they did have to think about what they wanted from their lives and they did everything they could to present themselves positively.'
>
> Suzy: 'Yeah, well I bet they've all got good grades. I'm too old now to go back to school and get any qualifications. Who's going to want to take me on? A criminal record and no qualifications. Looks great, doesn't it? Even if there were any jobs, which there aren't, I'd stand no chance!'
>
> Jeff: 'There's a couple of things in what you said there. You talk about being too old to go back to school, and you may be right. But there are other options for you to continue your education and improve on your grades. Can you think what they might be? For example, I'm wondering about college …?' (*Reflecting Suzy's feelings and sharing information to help her see that there are other options for her*)

In the example above, Jeff uses information in order to help Suzy to reframe her thinking and encourage her to feel that she is not alone and has some reason to remain positive. Jeff is tentative in his approach and tries to keep Suzy engaged in the process. For example, he reassures her that what she is feeling is what others in her situation also experience. This normalises her response and tackles her isolation. He helps her to reframe her thinking by asking how she might continue her education. He offers the example of a college course as a starting point for more in-depth exploration of a range of possible options, thus suggesting a more positive future scenario. Of course, it is likely to take more than this to enable Suzy to feel positive about her future. Jeff will need to draw on a range of skills in his work with Suzy, including challenge and immediacy, which will be explored later in this chapter. But using information in the right way can provide more than simply facts, figures, suggestions and directions. Culley and Bond (2011) offer a checklist for sharing information effectively. This includes:

- Ensuring relevance of the information shared – Is the information needed now? Does the client already have access to this information?
- Avoiding bombarding or overloading with information – share information in 'bite-sized chunks', minimising the possibility of clients taking on little or nothing of what has been shared.
- Presenting information clearly – avoid the use of jargon or complex terminology that is unhelpful and unnecessary and may serve to confuse or alienate clients.

- Inviting clients to summarise the information – ask clients to share their understanding of the information that has been offered. This helps to ensure clarity, and any misconceptions or misinterpretations can be addressed.
- Enabling clients to act on or use the information – the information, in itself, is not an end point, but a beginning. It is how it is acted upon that is important and it is the responsibility of the helper to enable clients to explore how they will use the information they have.
- Avoiding confusion between information sharing and advice giving – the former is a helpful and objective activity; the latter may involve giving your opinion or suggesting a course of action. Caution should be exercised wherever this may be the case in order to ensure that the ownership for decision making resides with the client.

Activity: Experiencing information sharing

Next time you seek help (it might be a doctor's appointment, a trip to the travel agent or a financial adviser, or even a conversation with a friend or family member regarding a decision you have to make), reflect on the way in which any information is shared with you. What did the 'helper' do that made the process a 'shared' activity? What could they have done differently in order to engage you more actively in the process?

It is important to remember that it is the interpretation and exploration of the information that is most helpful to clients. Having information and using it effectively are two quite different things. The role of the helper – counsellor, coach or mentor – is to focus on how their client can use it. By maintaining that focus, the helper is more likely to 'share' rather than 'give' information. It might be helpful to take a look at Case Study 4 in Part II; the community drugs and alcohol worker shares information effectively with her client, ensuring that at all times responsibility about how the information is used remains with her client.

Challenge

The process of challenge is central to effective helping and, like information sharing, it consists of a complex set of skills that should be used with care and sensitivity. The word 'challenge' can, in itself, be problematic. There are connotations here of confrontation, disapproval and negativity, none of which has a place in the helping process.

Culley and Bond remind us that 'to challenge means to question, to create doubt, to stimulate and to arouse' (2011: 104). In other words, challenge is a helpful and enabling process that engenders deeper reflection and thoughtfulness and can offer new perspectives and options for clients. Challenge is not about saying 'no' to clients, disagreeing or chastising, but rather about encouraging them to recognise and explore their feelings, options and actions in depth. Katrina is employed as head of pastoral care, working in a school. She explains her understanding of challenge in her work with pupils.

Case study: Katrina (head of pastoral care) – the process and skills of challenge

I learned about the skills of challenge when I trained as a mentor, before becoming head of pastoral care in the school. They seem particularly tricky to apply in a school environment when students are used to having their attitudes or behaviour in class challenged in ways that they sometimes find unhelpful or unfair by teachers. I see my role in supporting pupils and challenging them as different. I have learned that I can only challenge once I have built a relationship of trust and respect with students. And I try to remember to encourage them to challenge themselves, so I might say something like 'What do you think your teacher thought when you did that?' rather than 'Your teacher must have been very angry when you behaved like that'; or 'How could you approach this conversation differently with your mum?' rather than 'You need to stop being so rude to your mum.' I suppose, when I think about it, that I use questions – more than anything else – as a way to encourage students to challenge themselves and reflect on their thoughts, feelings and actions. I hadn't really thought of it in that way before.'

Katrina reminds us that 'challenge' is not necessarily a skill in itself, but rather a process that requires the use of a range of helping skills. Katrina explains here, that open and hypothetical questions can be used effectively to challenge clients to think in different ways and identify new perspectives. Detailed below are other skills (in addition to helpful questions) which can also be used to promote challenge. Examples are provided here to illustrate and illuminate each skill being used in order to challenge.

- *Helpful questions* – as illustrated above, asking open and hypothetical questions can serve to challenge a client to think about realism, consequences and discrepancies in their thoughts, feelings and actions.
  - o Counsellor: 'What do you think might happen if you tell your sister that you feel that way about her?'
- *Reflection* – (as explored in Chapter 3) restating a key, powerful word used by a client gives pause and the opportunity for them to

hear that word back, reflect and challenge the real meaning behind the word they selected.

- o   Counsellor: 'So you say that you *hate* your dad ...'

- *Summarising or paraphrasing* – (as explored in Chapter 3), summarising what your client has told you, their words, thoughts, feelings and actions, provides clients with an opportunity to reflect again on what they have said. This can be particularly helpful if there are contradictions evident in the content that clients are sharing. A summary will reflect these contradictions back to the client and challenge them to make sense of or 'unpick' the contradictions in their thoughts, feelings and actions.

- o   Coach: 'So you say you feel held back in your job at the moment and you don't see any future for you in the company where you work. You also explain that your manager has encouraged you to apply for promotion within the company and to access continuing professional development opportunities that are available. I guess I'm curious about that ...'

- *Information sharing* – sometimes helpers can use information to make the challenge, thus leaving themselves free to support the client once they have understood the implications of the information. In the example below, the learning mentor is letting the information challenge the client rather than saying 'No, that's not possible' themselves.

- o   Mentor: 'You explain that you want to use the library to prepare for your assignment this weekend? Let's just check on the website when the library is open ...'

- *Immediacy* – this skill will be explored in depth later in this chapter. Simply put, immediacy is about dealing with the underlying feelings that are present in the here and now in a helping relationship. By using immediacy, clients are enabled to challenge and explore what they are really thinking and feeling.

- o   Counsellor: 'You are describing something that has happened to you that sounds very painful and sad. Yet as you talk, you laugh and seem to suggest that these things weren't important or difficult for you at the time ...?'

- *Silence* – like immediacy, the skill of silence will be explored later in this chapter. Silence can be used to challenge by simply providing a space for clients to reflect on the meaning behind the words they have spoken.

- o   Client: 'I feel sick ... (silence) ... sick and hurt ... (silence) ... just desperately, desperately sad, I suppose, and maybe guilty too ... (silence) ... Yes, I think it's the guilt that I feel most strongly.'

To challenge another human being, even in the context of a helping relationship, can be damaging if not done with sensitivity. Culley and Bond's (2004) guidelines for effective challenging are detailed in Reid and Westergaard's text (2011: 54) on effective counselling with young people:

- *Be tentative, not confrontational* – use language that conveys a 'hunch' or a 'feeling' rather than a fact when you challenge.
- *Keep the aims of the challenge in mind* – remember that challenge is all about helping clients to explore and reassess, not about telling young people what to do!
- *Make sure that the client is able to 'hear' and understand the challenge* – clients in a highly emotional or vulnerable state may not be resilient enough to accept a challenge for what is (a helpful and positive intervention); alternatively they may defend against it or reject the challenger.
- *Keep the challenge close to the client's perspective* – do not offer something as a challenge that is alien to the young person's understanding. Find a different way of posing the challenge that makes sense to the client.
- *Be concrete and specific* – make clear to the young person exactly what the challenge refers to. This does not contradict the earlier suggestion of 'being tentative', but rather focuses on the need to be clear and unambiguous when it comes to challenging.
- *Avoid finding fault or blaming* – always challenge from a 'no-blame' position. Blaming leads to defensiveness and is contrary to the core conditions of a person-centred approach.
- *Encourage self-challenge* – the most effective challenges are those that young people pose for themselves. The use of the skill of summarising can help clients to self-challenge.
- *Be open to challenge* – a counsellor who is defensive about their approach to counselling and unable or unwilling to hear a client's challenge is not well placed to encourage young people to accept challenges themselves.

I would like to offer three additional points to consider when challenging clients:

- *Earn the right to challenge* – only once a relationship of trust has developed can a challenge be received and responded to effectively.
- *Do not 'over-do' challenge* – however effectively done, being continuously challenged can be exhausting. Helpers need to be aware of timing challenges in a helpful and constructive way and, perhaps, 'parking' some challenges for later.
- *Explain why you are challenging* – an explanation of why you are challenging the client can help to reduce possible confusion and alleviate feelings of defensiveness on behalf of the client in response to the challenge.

Later in the chapter, once we have explored the skills of immediacy and silence further, I will suggest an activity that will offer an opportunity to practise the process of challenge using the range of skills identified above. For now, the following activity invites you to reflect on your feelings about challenging clients.

Activity: How do you feel about challenge?

Try to identify two separate occasions where a challenge took place. The first is when you were challenged by someone (a family member, friend, colleague, teacher, counsellor or other) and the second is when you challenged someone else (the list above applies). Jot down your responses to the questions below:

1. How did you feel about receiving/making the challenge?
2. How appropriate was it to challenge? What was the rationale for the challenge in each case?
3. How effectively was the challenge delivered in each case?
4. How could the challenge have been delivered more effectively in each case?

It is important that we become aware of our own responses to challenge. We may have poor experiences of being challenged and will therefore regard all challenges as a criticism. This could mean that we avoid challenging clients for fear that they will feel we are criticising them. Alternatively, we may be very confident, self-aware and secure in our own emotions and regard challenges as a welcome way to learn and develop. But we cannot assume that all our clients are at this point, and therefore we must ensure that the approach we take to challenge is both sensitive and tentative. Take a look at Case Study 6 in Part II to see how effectively the manager of a children's home challenges her young client.

Immediacy

The skill of immediacy was outlined very briefly above, as it can be used as an effective tool to challenge clients to reflect more deeply on what and how they are feeling. When first introduced to the skill of immediacy, helpers often assume that it means dealing with the most pressing issue that the client is presenting, as quickly as possible. This is not surprising as that is what the term 'immediacy' suggests. In fact, immediacy in the helping context means something quite specific – and slightly different to that interpretation. Culley and Bond (2011) explain that helping interventions take place in the present, although what is discussed is often focused on the past or the future. They suggest that there are times when it can be helpful to stay with what is happening in the present, in the room between helper and client, to illuminate and address clients' underlying emotions. The example of immediacy below shows Steve, a counsellor, working with Gary, a young man who has lost the use of his legs as a result of a car accident.

Case study: Steve (counsellor) and Gary – using immediacy

Gary: (*With a shrug and a laugh*) 'Look, hey, I know I'm crippled. No point in moaning about it. Just got to get on with it. Ha! I even get to travel around in this little beauty (*Patting his wheelchair*). What more could a bloke ask for, eh?'

Steve: 'That sounds a very light-hearted response to something that has affected your life so deeply.'

Gary: 'Yeah well, what do you expect me to do? Sit here and cry for an hour? That's not me, mate. That's not how I operate.'

Steve: 'I can see how important it is for you to remain positive and focused on the future. But I also think that there's something about the way you're expressing how you feel that shows me how angry and sad you feel deep down. Have I got that right?'

Gary: (*Laughing*) 'Angry? What's the point of that? It won't bring my legs back, will it?'

Steve: 'No, it won't. But I guess what I'm picking up is that you are feeling deeply angry and sad, and what I want to say to you is that there is no need to try to hide those feelings here with me. This is a place where you can be safe enough to express how you really feel.'

Gary: (*Silence... and then, spoken softly*) 'Of course I'm angry. I'm so, so fucking angry. What do you expect? (*Begins to sob*) But I can't show that, can I? If I start showing people how I really feel, I'll never stop crying. No way. I can't be like this, be weak in front of my mates. No way.'

The example above illustrates that immediacy is a very powerful, but difficult, skill to use effectively. Here Steve is picking up a strong sense that Gary's words and his emotions are incongruent. In other words, he is saying one thing, but feeling quite different underneath. It might be argued that in a case such as this, Gary is managing his pain effectively by putting a 'bright face' on his situation. This may well be a useful strategy to adopt, in order to manage this traumatic change in his circumstances outside the counselling room, but the purpose of counselling is to enable clients to express what they are truly feeling without holding back for fear of another person's response. There may be implications in the long term if Gary suppresses the true extent of his anger and emotional pain; counselling, as Steve suggests, should offer him a safe space to talk about and work through how he really feels.

Culley and Bond (2011) highlight key points in counselling when immediacy might be helpful:

- *Trust* – some clients may not engage in the helping process because either they feel that they are unable to fully trust the helper or they find it difficult to form, or fear forming, trusting relationships. Approaching this lack of trust by using immediacy will mean that the focus initially remains on creating a trusting relationship. Only once this relationship is in place can the client begin to engage in and benefit fully from the helping process.
- *Circular helping* – sometimes the content of helping interventions appears to be going round in circles without clients seeming to move on or make any progress. Where this is the case, the helper can use immediacy to share their thoughts about what is happening in the 'here and now' in the helping relationship in order to discover what is blocking progress.
- *Boundaries of the helping relationship* – it is important that the relationship between helper and client is boundaried (discussed in depth in Chapter 7). Clients and helpers need to be clear about the nature and remit of the helping relationship. They are not friends, but are engaged in a professional helping relationship. Therefore clients are likely to know very little about their helper – client, coach or mentor. Where helpers feel that their clients are expecting or seeking a different kind of relationship, then they have a responsibility to use immediacy to highlight their feelings about what is happening in the helping relationship in order to reinforce the boundaries.

To these I would add:

- *Tension* – when the helper senses that there is an unspoken but nevertheless very real tension between themselves and their client, for example: if a client appears to feel angry about something that the helper has said, but does not express this verbally.
- *Heightened emotions* – when the helper senses that the client is trying to 'manage' or suppress an emotion (see the example of Gary

and Steve, above) where it would be useful to name, express and explore the underlying feelings openly.

- *Changes in demeanour* – where clients' facial expressions or body postures change, for example '... and as you said that, your face lit up.'
- *Projection* – when the client is projecting their own feelings onto the helper. For example, the client may say 'I know you think I'm stupid' or 'You must think I'm mad.' Here the helper should enable the client to 'unpick' these projected feelings and understand where they come from and what they really mean to the client.
- *Feedback* – there may be times when a helper feels compelled to offer a client immediate feedback, for example: 'I just want us to pause for a moment so that you can hear me say how effectively I think you handled that situation.'
- *Challenge* – as explained earlier in this chapter, immediacy can serve to act as a challenge by examining what is happening in the 'here and now' between the helper and the client.

Although of course the helper is always present in any intervention with clients, the focus is, for the most part, fixed on the client and helping them to tell and explore their story and make decisions about changes they want to make in their lives. Where helpers select to use the skill of immediacy, they are bringing themselves firmly into the interaction. The 'I' word is seldom used by helpers, but it is always present when we use immediacy. Typical responses by a helper using immediacy include:

- 'I get the feeling that ...'
- 'I'm wondering if you feel that ...'
- 'I wonder why I'm feeling that ...'
- 'I feel there might be something else going on here.'
- 'I'm getting the feeling that something I just said is making you feel angry/sad/frustrated/uncomfortable.'
- 'When you said that, a moment ago, I felt quite frightened.'

It's important to notice that, in each of the examples above, the language used is tentative and the helper is 'checking out' rather than asserting. Immediacy is a skill that some helpers may avoid. It can feel 'risky' and some may fear that by using the skill they could 'unlock' potentially painful and difficult feelings in the client. This may be true but, if it is, it is because those painful and difficult feelings exist – and the helping relationship should be one where, if the client is able, those emotions can be explored and managed.

Activity: Your response to immediacy

Take a moment to reflect on what I have said about using the skill of immediacy. What are your thoughts about how useful it might be to seek to address clients' underlying fears and feelings? What challenges do you think you may experience in using the skill?

The final activity in this chapter should offer you the opportunity to try out the skill of immediacy in a safe space. Remember that it is an advanced skill, and one that many experienced helpers still find challenging to use, even though they know how powerful the outcomes can be for clients. Case Study 1 in Part II illustrates the skill of immediacy being used by a learning support assistant in a school setting.

Silence

It may surprise you to see the skill of silence explored under the heading 'Advanced Skills'. After all, the skill of silence is all about being quiet. Surely that is not difficult to achieve? I want to begin with an activity in order for you to reflect on your own response to silence.

Activity: How do I feel about silence?

Using a scale of 1–10 (1 being 'Very uncomfortable', 10 being 'Totally at ease'), how would you rate your ability to remain silent in the following situations?

- A close family member is upset and crying because of a recent breakdown in a relationship.
- You are at a team meeting and your manager asks which team member would be willing to take the minutes.
- You are out with friends and conversation runs dry.
- You are watching television with a close friend or partner.
- And finally, list the people in your life who you would feel comfortable to sit with in a room in silence.

Our responses to silence are very personal. Some may feel comfortable with silence, others may not. In the examples above, some of us may feel compelled to 'rescue' the close family member who is upset, and tell them that 'all will be fine', whilst others may be comfortable to sit as a witness to their pain. In the case of minute-taking in the team meeting, some may find themselves offering to take the minutes even though they do not particularly want to do so, because the silence feels so uncomfortable to them, whilst others may feel that they could remain silent all day rather than offer to take the minutes! The point here is that it is important to acknowledge that silence can be a very useful tool in a helping interaction, and we need to develop a way in which we, as helpers, can be comfortable with silence ourselves, in order to make it work where appropriate in helping interventions.

The nature of a helping relationship suggests that those who choose to become helpers have done so because they want to try to make things better for people who are experiencing challenges or even pain in their lives. We have to understand, though, that the power to make change resides with clients. We cannot make assurances that all will be well. We simply do not know that. Sometimes the imperative to use words, when someone we are with is in pain, is so strong that the helper may risk making statements that cannot be guaranteed, because it is too painful for them to witness and contain someone else's grief. Where a helper feels compelled to say 'It will be fine', 'Don't worry, it will all work out for the best', or 'Trust me. I know it will be OK', they should pause and consider using the time more productively in silence to listen to and stay with another's pain.

So, why might we want to use silence in counselling, coaching or mentoring interventions? Culley and Bond explain:

> Listening to and using silences creatively in using counselling skills means effecting an appropriate balance between (a) enabling clients, (b) providing a space for them to reflect and (c) helping them to face their discomfort. (2011: 32)

It may be disingenuous to see silence as 'enabling' (as Culley and Bond suggest) but, actually, providing a pause can encourage clients to think more deeply, reflect and explore their feelings effectively. A hurried question or intervention from the helper may serve to interrupt or divert a client's train of thought and take them in a different and possibly less helpful direction. As stated earlier, often questions are used when the helper senses their client's discomfort and feels compelled to rescue them. Culley and Bond offer a different perspective, suggesting here that silence may enable a client to face their own discomfort, by sending a message that the helper is not 'overwhelmed' by what the client is experiencing and that this is a safe space to explore difficult feelings. The example below serves to illustrate the use of silence; Gloria, a counsellor, stays with her client Samuel's pain.

Case study: Gloria (counsellor) and Samuel – using silence in the helping relationship

Gloria: 'You seem very sad today, Samuel. Very quiet and very sad.'
(*Silence ... After a while Samuel hides his head in his hands ... silence ... Samuel begins to cry, quietly ... silence ... Samuel wipes his eyes on his sleeve and takes deep breaths ... silence ... and then, after some moments of silence ...*)

Gloria: 'What's going on for you right now, Samuel? What are you feeling?'
(*Silence ... Samuel, head down, begins to speak very softly.*)

Samuel: 'I just can't bear it. I can't bear how this feels any longer ... I don't really know how to describe it' ... (*Silence ...*) 'It just hurts so much, I suppose' ... (*Silence ...*) 'I just can't pretend any more that everything is OK.'

In the above example, Gloria provides a space in which Samuel can express his emotions freely. She does not rush him, or try to 'jolly him along', or minimise the significance of his response, but rather she respects the depth of his feelings and, when she does make an intervention, she simply asks him what is going on for him in order that he can begin to articulate and explore how he feels.

It can be difficult to use silence in a helping intervention, and equally challenging to know what to say to interrupt a silence. There are two helpful ways to interrupt a silence. First, there will be times when the helper may simply want to reflect on what they have observed, for example: 'You seemed to be deep in thought just then and I noticed that your hands were tensed into fists', or 'It felt then as though you were trying hard to make sense of something really important to you.' Second, the helper may decide to break the silence with a question, as in the example with Gloria and Samuel above. Questions might include: 'I wonder what you are feeling right now?'; 'What are you thinking about?'; or 'What is going around in your head at the moment?'

Like the other advanced skills introduced in this chapter, silence takes practice and should be used mindfully, not just as an enforced measure because the helper feels immobilised and cannot think how to respond. Take this opportunity to read Case Studies 9 and 10 in Part II. Both helpers use silence very effectively in their work with their respective clients.

The activity below brings the concepts explored in this chapter together and offers you an opportunity to consider how you might use these skills in practice in the following helping intervention. In addition to focusing on the skills, remember that the core conditions of empathy, congruence and unconditional positive regard should under-pin everything you do and will inform the 'tone' of your practice. If you are already working with clients, you may want to think about asking a client's permission to record an intervention, play it back, and ana-lyse your use of skills – foundation and advanced – throughout.

Activity: Case study/role play

Read through the following case study and identify where and how you would use advanced skills. If possible, ask a friend or colleague to role-play this (or another case study of your own devising) with you. At the end of the role play, ask the 'client' how it felt to be challenged, to experience silence and immediacy, and to consider any information needs. How did it feel for you, as helper? What might you need to develop further?

Harbinder is a young woman who has come to see you because she is feeling trapped in a job she started when she left school. You have met together on five occasions; Harbinder has opened up and explained that she not only is unsatisfied in her job, but also feels trapped in a relationship with her boyfriend, who she has been with since leaving school. She cares for him, but is feeling attracted to someone else at work. Today, Harbinder is visibly upset. Two things have happened: the first is that she has seen an advert for a job that she is interested in, and the second is that when she talked about this to her boyfriend, they argued. He wants her to stay where she is for now, 'because soon we will be married, and then we can start a family and it won't matter where you work'. As she explains this to you, Harbinder begins to cry.

I hope that you were able to engage fully in this activity, either using the suggested case study or your own role play. Opportunities to share infor-mation, challenge and use immediacy and silence, in addition to practising the foundation skills of counselling, are likely to come through role-play activities initially. In the helping professions, counsellors, coaches and mentors will find themselves accessing a range of skills in order to work effectively with clients, but at all times they should be mindful of what they are doing and be clear about their rationale for using the skills they are applying throughout the intervention.

Summary

This chapter has focused on the definition and application of a range of advanced counselling skills used by counsellors, coaches and mentors in helping relationships. The skills identified here, together with the key skills explored in Chapter 3, will enable helpers to work effectively with their clients, build relationships of trust, explore issues in depth, consider and evaluate a range of possible options available to them, and identify specific action steps that clients may decide they want to take. It is important to remind ourselves that these skills are used most effectively within an integrative approach – whereby the core conditions of person-centred practice underpin our relationships with clients at all times, whilst a model for effective integration is used in order to keep our work focused and purposeful.

Further reading suggestions

(As for Chapter 3, but with one addition.)

Culley, S. and Bond, B. (2011) *Integrative Counselling Skills in Action* (3rd edn). London: Sage – A must-have text for anyone who is training or embarking on practice in the helping professions.

Geldard, K. and Geldard, G. (2005) *Practical Counselling Skills: An Integrative Approach*. London: Palgrave Macmillan – A book crammed with helpful suggestions for activities to develop counselling skills.

Nelson-Jones, R. (2012) *Basic Counselling Skills: A Helper's Manual* (3rd edn). London: Sage – A clearly written and engaging book that describes a range of counselling skills and techniques.

van Nieuwerburgh, C. (2014) *An Introduction to Coaching Skills: A Practical Guide*. London: Sage – An excellent resource with an accompanying website which gives specific examples of skills used in coaching practice.

5

SKILLS IN CONTEXT

Chapter objectives: Readers will have the opportunity to ...

- identify key processes in helping relationships;
- consider how helping skills are used to establish a contract for helping sessions;
- examine the importance of agreeing an agenda for helping interventions;
- reflect on how helping skills are used to enable goal setting;
- identify how helping skills are applied in the action planning process.

Introduction

The previous two chapters focused on developing a range of skills necessary to engage in helping interventions with clients – counselling, coaching and mentoring. When foundation helping skills are used effectively, whilst adhering to the core conditions of empathy, congruence and unconditional positive regard (see Chapters 2 and 3), the helper is able to develop a relationship of trust with their client. Once the trusting relationship is established, helpers can access advanced skills (see Chapter 4) in order to challenge and enable greater reflection. Advanced skills can assist the client to tell their story, reflect on how they might want their lives to be different, focus on the options available to them, and make decisions about the best option for them. This process leads to considering realistic plans for change and to putting those plans in action. This may sound like an unstructured and organic process, and to some extent that is true. Interactions should always be flexible in order to respond to clients' immediate needs. However, to ensure flexibility whilst also working towards positive change, the application of a structured approach which involves key processes is helpful. Chapter 2 introduces just such a structured approach – Egan's three-stage helping model – and provides an overview of the model. What follows here are the micro-processes which helpers should be aware of and apply: the key elements within the model which are necessary to ensure that helping interventions remain purposeful and focused.

This chapter will explore four key processes:

- Contracting
- Agenda setting
- Goal setting
- Action planning

Each process forms an integral part of a helping intervention and is what sets 'helping' conversations apart from any other kind of interaction. Normally, when we engage in conversation with family, friends or colleagues, we do not set an agenda for the conversation, or identify and reflect on goals we want to achieve as a result of the conversation, or plan action to be implemented after the conversation. By contrast, those elements should be at the heart of any helping intervention. This chapter will explore each process in detail, taking a broadly 'chronological' approach by beginning with contracting and agenda setting, then moving on to goal setting and finally action planning.

Contracting

The concept of 'contracting' in helping relationships can be confusing. This is because there are two distinct contracting processes: one at the start of the relationship where client and helper meet for the first time and agree how they will work together, and one at the start of every helping intervention where client and helper work together to agree an agenda for that session. We will examine both definitions of contracting, but from now on, when I use the word 'contracting' I will be referring to the initial process when client and helper are meeting for the first time, whilst the term 'agreeing an agenda' will be applied to the process that should happen early in every subsequent session when client and helper meet together.

At the outset, it is important that clients entering into counselling, coaching and mentoring relationships understand fully the nature of the helping they are about to receive – what it is and what it is not – before deciding whether or not to engage in the activity. Many people seek help at points in their lives when they are feeling vulnerable, anxious, fearful or upset. They may be looking for advice, reassurance or even answers. It is precisely for this reason that clients should be made aware of the nature of the helping relationship and the role of the helper. Advice giving, providing reassurance and suggesting answers are not functions of helping relationships. Rather it is the responsibility of clients, with the support of the helper, to advise and reassure themselves and to find their own answers to the questions they are posing. Ewan, a bereavement counsellor, explains the need for an agreement about what counselling is in his work.

Case study: Ewan (bereavement counsellor) talks about contracting

When I first meet clients, they are usually trying to deal with overwhelming emotions. They are often feeling sad, angry, bereft, lonely, hopeless and sometimes even guilty. These are powerful emotions which clients find almost unbearable to experience and manage in their everyday lives: that's why they've come to counselling in the first place. But it is important for them to be aware that counselling does not involve a magic wand which I, the counsellor, will wave in the air so that all their pain disappears in a puff of smoke – quite the contrary. Counselling will often be a painful and difficult process which, ultimately, can lead to change and some kind of resolution, but this may take time to achieve. I make it clear that I do not own a magic wand, but that I can help them to explore, verbalise and reflect on their feelings in a safe and confidential space. With me they are free to say the 'unsayable'. I explain that this process is likely to take time. Some clients come once and never return, once they understand what counselling is all about. They realise that it is not for them, at this time. People have to make their own decisions about what they are letting themselves in for. And they can only do that if they are clear about what the process entails.

Helpers use the skill of information sharing (see Chapter 4) to develop their clients' understanding of counselling, coaching or mentoring. This means ensuring that a dialogue between helper and client takes place. We will examine this in more detail later. Once clients have become aware of the nature of the helping process, they are then free to decide whether or not this is likely to be appropriate or useful for them. In some cases, of course, clients are referred for counselling, coaching or mentoring, perhaps with little choice in the matter. In cases such as these, it is just as important – perhaps more so – to be clear about the process of helping, and to take time to share information carefully with clients so that expectations, and any resistance, are managed effectively.

If clients decide that they do want to enter into a helping relationship with their counsellor, coach or mentor, then a more formal agreement about what the process involves – the practicalities and the nature of the relationship – must be agreed. This process is termed 'contracting' and requires the use of more information sharing on behalf of the helper.

Activity: Contracting

Note down the key elements that you think should be featured in a helping contract. Think about the practicalities of the helping process (for example record keeping) as well as the features of the relationship (for example confidentiality).

Jenkins (2007) has identified some important items that might be included in a counselling contract. His list below applies to counsellors working in private practice or for organisations where clients pay for their therapy. Nevertheless, aside from the first point, the list can equally be applied to those who work in funded or voluntary counselling, coaching or mentoring contexts.

- *Cost* – what is the cost of each session, if applicable?
- *Duration and frequency* – how long will the session be and how often will sessions take place? A counselling 'hour' is normally 50 minutes long. However, coaching and mentoring sessions may vary in length and there is possibly less rigidity and more flexibility for agreeing timings. Meetings may be once a week at the same time and the same place, or may be more flexible.
- *Arrangements for cancellations* – again, in paid sessions, cancellations by the client may be charged. It might also be that clients cannot cancel on more than one or two occasions without risking terminating the relationship. This must be made very clear if it is the case. Generally it is important for the helper to show reliability and consistency and 'mirror' this professional approach to their client. Therefore cancellations on the part of the helper should be avoided if at all possible, but where this is unavoidable, as much notice as possible should be given.
- *Main characteristics of therapy* – again, this applies specifically to counselling, where the counsellor will discuss the theoretical

orientation of their approach, for example cognitive behavioural, person-centred or integrative. That said, mentors and coaches will also explain how they work and the purpose of the helping relationship in the contracting stage.

- *Number of sessions and arrangements for review* – it is always helpful to identify an initial number of sessions (normally four or six) and agree that a review will take place on the fourth or sixth session, to discuss the client's feelings about the process and to determine whether it should continue. If so, then a further number of sessions will be agreed before another review takes place. This serves to reassure clients and enables them to feel 'safe', as they know that the helping relationship is not simply going to terminate unexpectedly without notice.
- *Confidentiality* – this will be discussed fully in Chapter 7. It is important that both client and helper are clear about the boundaries of the relationship, record keeping and the times when the helper may be required to break confidentiality (if the client or others are at risk of significant harm, for example).
- *Terminating therapy* – agreeing reasons for when the relationship might come to an end and sharing what the ending process is likely to involve.
- *Cover in case of illness* – being clear about whether another helper is likely to intervene on a temporary basis if the counsellor, coach or mentor has a prolonged period of absence.
- *Date and signature of both parties.*

Not all helping relationships will be governed by a formal, written contract signed by both parties. Nevertheless, the points made above are a useful guide as to what needs to be discussed in order that both helper and client are clear, on a number of practical and procedural issues, before entering into a helping relationship. Even if it appears that the helping relationship is very informal and flexible – a peer mentor, for example – it is important that both helper and client are clear about issues such as confidentiality, in order to feel safe and to build a relationship of openness and trust. Zachary, when explaining the contracting phase in mentoring, suggests that contracting is a central process:

> The outcome of this phase is a mentoring partnership work plan anchored in well-defined goals, measurements for success, delineation of mutual responsibility, accountability mechanisms, and protocols for dealing with stumbling blocks. (2000: 93)

Time taken at the initial stage of the relationship to clarify these points will help to ensure that effective engagement takes place and that confusion, problems and issues later are avoided.

Entering into a contract – whether formal or informal – is an important process that should take place in the first helping intervention, but should not need to be revisited subsequently unless issues arise which require further clarification. It is worth sounding a note of caution here regarding the contracting process. Clients have come to see you because they need help and support of some kind. They may have plucked up the courage to make an appointment and may want to tell their story as soon as they are able. Entering into a lengthy speech or information-giving session on your part is not helpful. Helpers should be mindful about the skill of information sharing and ensure that, as far as possible, this discussion is just that – a discussion, not a monologue. Clients' expectations, thoughts and feelings are encouraged to be shared throughout the process, with the use of open questions, summary and reflecting back. Case Studies 2, 3 and 7 in Part II all make reference to the importance of contracting in the helping relationship.

The other activity which is often termed 'contracting' that takes place in helping relationships, as explained earlier in the chapter, is referred to here as 'agreeing an agenda'.

Agreeing an agenda

Unlike contracting, outlined above, which takes place mostly at the initial counselling appointment, agreeing an agenda is an activity which is a crucial part of *every* helping interaction. The helper will not know what is likely to form the focus of discussions for the session until the client tells them what they would like to explore. So in the early stages of each interaction, it is helpful to ask the client how they would like to use the time you have together. There are a number of reasons for this:

- The client will develop a more reflective approach and will use the time between and before sessions to think about the issues they would like to explore when they next see you. Thus the work continues outside the immediate 'helping' context.
- Early on in the session, the client can prioritise which issues they would like to talk about. They may identify two or three things that they would like to focus on during the session. By asking the open question, 'Where would you like to start?', the client has the opportunity to order their thoughts and take responsibility for how they would like to use the time.
- The helper has the opportunity to assist the client to be realistic about the time available. If the client identifies ten things they would like to talk about, the helper may suggest that time could run short. This will ensure that clients' expectations about what can be achieved in each session are realistic.

- Agreeing an agenda early on in each session will mitigate against the client waiting until the session ends to say, 'Of course, what I really wanted to talk about today was ... but I didn't get the chance.'

Agreeing an agenda does not mean sitting the client down, asking them what they want to talk about, and then working through each point systematically, without deviation. This implies a somewhat mechanistic and inflexible approach – and goes against the ethos of integrative practice underpinned by person-centred core conditions. Rather, by using open questions to encourage the client to 'tell their story' and identify the issues that are 'around' or 'present' for them during the beginning phase of the interaction, an agenda can be agreed for the remainder of the session which identifies areas for deeper reflection. It may be that the client, whilst exploring the first item on the agenda, discovers an issue, thought or feeling which emerges or is illuminated and they want to reflect on this further. It is not the responsibility of the helper to say, 'Stop! I'm very sorry but we won't have time to cover anything else if you keep talking about this!' Instead the helper will be actively listening and attending to the needs of their client. The time should be used flexibly and, if there is an appropriate moment, the helper may gently encourage their client to reflect on how they are using the session and, if necessary, review the agenda and make changes accordingly.

Some clients, particularly younger clients or those who have been referred or 'sent' for help, may find it difficult to identify issues for discussion. Here, the helper can offer broad or generic examples of issues that individuals may bring. This is not suggesting or dictating an agenda, but simply helping the client to understand ways in which the time together may be used.

Cameron (2008) describes helping interventions as 'interviews'. When talking about the importance of defining the purpose and scope of each counselling interview early in every intervention, she suggests asking clients to describe what they hope to achieve from the session. She explains that:

> This reinforces the idea that the interview is goal focused and that there can be achievable outcomes from it, with relevance to the client and their issues. This opening question might be worded: 'If this interview goes well for you, what do you hope you will gain from it?' (2008: 92)

Agreeing an agenda is a challenging activity, and one that those new to the helping professions can find daunting. Common pitfalls might include:

- agreeing an agenda too early in the interaction, without sufficient understanding of the client's needs and issues;
- 'running with' the first issue that the client raises and then not having time to focus on other issues that are perhaps equally, or even more, important;

• imposing an agenda based on the client's last session, whereby the helper 'suggests' areas to follow up, when actually the client has 'moved on' and other issues have become more significant in their lives.

In the example below, Tom, the career coach, has met his client Ellie on four previous occasions. They have spent the first ten minutes of their fifth session agreeing an agenda, whereby Ellie has talked about how she's feeling today and identified a range of issues that are around for her. What follows is an example of Tom's use of the skill of summarising (see Chapter 3), where the main agenda points are checked out with Ellie.

Case study: Tom (career coach) and Ellie – agreeing an agenda

Tom: 'OK, Ellie. It sounds as though this week has been a particularly tough one for you. And since we last met a few things have happened that have really got you thinking about your future. From what you say, it sounds as though you would like to go over some of the areas we've talked about before and also explore some new thoughts you've had. So – and stop me if I've got this wrong – you'd like to talk about an incident at work this week with your line manager; you also think it would be useful to go back to something we talked about last time regarding the possibility of returning to education and perhaps studying for a degree. And then you'd like to reflect on how you can share your thoughts about your future career ideas with your partner, who is anxious about some of the changes you are planning. Have I got that right?'

Ellie: (*Nodding enthusiastically*) 'Yes, yes, absolutely. Spot on.'

Tom: 'OK then ... where would you like to start?'

Ellie: 'Umm ... I think the incident with my line manager would be good to talk about first. It feels so raw and it's very fresh in my mind.'

Tom: 'OK ... And then?'

Ellie: 'Umm ... maybe ... umm ... yes, I know: how about going back to what we talked about last time? You know, the education stuff, and then the stuff that's going on at home with Chris.'

Tom: 'That's great. And you know, of course Ellie, that if other things come up, like they have before in sessions, that's fine. But this is our starting point. Is that OK?'

There are opposing thoughts on whether or not note taking is appropriate in helping interventions. Often the taking of notes serves to detract from, rather than enhance, active listening. However, at the agenda agreement stage, it can be helpful to jot down the agenda 'items'. Using the example above, Tom might write:

- Line manager
- Education
- Partner

This will serve to act as a reminder of the three key areas that have been identified as the interaction progresses, and helps to keep both Tom and Ellie focused on how they agreed the time should be used.

Activity: Agreeing an agenda

Ask a friend, colleague or fellow student if they will engage in a role-play activity, playing the part of a client in a helping intervention. Begin by deciding on the professional context – counselling, coaching or mentoring – and decide how many times you have already seen this client. If you decide that this is a first session, you can also work through the 'contracting' stage, before going on to 'agree an agenda' for the session. The 'client' should bring a number of issues in order that these can be discussed initially and then an agenda for the session agreed. If you are already in practice in a helping context, you do not need to undertake a role play, but do take time to reflect on how your sessions begin and how effectively an agenda is agreed.

It is worth making the distinction here between 'topics' for discussion and 'issues' to be discussed. A topic is a generic area, for example a couple who come for counselling to talk about their relationship; an issue is what is unique to the client – for example the couple are concerned about their lack of intimacy and the distance that seems to have opened up between them. It is the *issues* that should be identified at the agenda-setting stage, rather than a broad 'topic'. Case Study 2 in Part II illustrates the importance of agreeing an agenda at the start of each session for Maggie, who is seeing her life-coach.

Goal setting

Another key element of the helping process is the activity of goal setting. Like agenda agreement, goal setting is what sets a helping conversation apart from a social interaction. Helping professionals work alongside their clients to enable them to make positive change in their lives. In order to do this, clients must identify and explore the areas and issues that either are causing them concern or they want to change, before going on to think about how they would like things to be different in the future. It is the process of identifying a future scenario – stage 2 of Egan's model – that involves goal setting.

The GROW model (Whitmore, 1992) was developed for the coaching context; its name is an acronym where G = goal, R = reality, O = options, and W = will. The model is focused both on goal setting and on ensuring that the goals set are realistic and that the client has the will, determination and necessary resources to achieve them. Van Nieuwerburgh explains that 'at heart, coaching is an interaction that supports people to achieve goals' (2014: 72). Nelson-Jones, writing about helping in the counselling context, suggests that helpers should 'be very skilled at combining active listening skills with probes designed to clarify goals, explore options for attaining them and develop plans to implement a chosen option' (2012: 98). Garvey, Stokes and Megginson sound a cautionary note regarding goal setting in coaching and mentoring relationships, reminding us that there may be more than one agenda in play in these contexts, particularly where the coaching and mentoring have been provided by an employer in order to develop an employee's performance at work. Here, there may be tensions or even conflict concerning the goals of helping. Where this is the case, Garvey, Stokes and Megginson (2014: 178) suggest that helpers may want to ask themselves the following questions:

- Who dictates the agenda?
- Whose interests do the goals serve?
- Whose model of reality is privileged?
- How can the impact be measured?
- How can the usefulness of coaching and mentoring be focused?
- How can collusion be controlled?

They go on to suggest that both helper and client discuss these issues in order to understand and agree how they can work together to arrive at a deeper understanding and engage in informed decision making.

In spite of the cautionary note sounded above, there is significant agreement that goal setting is central to effective helping.

Activity: Goal setting

Take a moment to think about your own situation. Try to identify one or two goals that you would like to achieve. If you can, categorise these goals as short term (within the next six months), medium term (within the next year), and long term (within the next five years). Now write these goals down, as we will return to this activity later in the chapter when we consider options for achieving goals and explore the concept of action planning.

It is important to make the distinction between 'goal' and 'action'. The goal is *what* you would like to achieve; the action is *how* you will get there. In the testimony below, Ashraf, a student, talks about the goals he set for himself when working with his mentor at school. He does not identify the action that he took in order to achieve his goals, but setting the goal is the first step in the process.

Case study: Ashraf (school student) – goal setting

'When I met my mentor I wasn't sure what mentoring was all about. I didn't really know why I was seeing her, to be honest. But she talked to me about what mentoring was all about, and we started to meet regularly. Each time we did, we talked about what I wanted to work on and improve. So, for example, I said that I wanted to be a bit more organised and manage my time better. She explained that this could be one of my goals and then we thought about how I might go about achieving it. My big goal, long term, was to get good grades in my exams and then go on to university. So we agreed some immediate goals and some goals for the future. My mentor kept telling me that the goals had to be 'SMART'. I didn't know what she meant at first, but she explained how important it was that my goals are realistic and achievable. This helped to keep me focused and on track, I suppose.

Ashraf highlights the importance of identifying SMART goals:

- Specific
- Measurable
- Achievable
- Realistic
- Time-bound

It is important to ensure that clients are setting themselves goals that are realistic and achievable. If they are unable to be realistic about what they want to achieve, then they will feel demoralised when the goals are not realised. Nelson-Jones offers some helpful advice when supporting clients to identify goals. He explains:

> Avoid bombarding clients with questions about goals. In most instances, small is beautiful. A few well-chosen questions that get to the heart of what the client wants to achieve and avoid are all that is necessary. However, sometimes you may need to facilitate clients in exploring deeper goals and the values that underpin them rather than surface goals. In all instances, you should respect clients' rights to set their own goals and also intersperse active listening with questions to clarify goals. (2012: 99)

Nelson-Jones makes the distinction between 'deep' and 'surface' goals. This is helpful and serves to remind us that some goals may need more in-depth exploration than others. If we return to Ashraf's testimony above, we can see that wanting to improve his organisational skills is a 'surface' goal, whereas going to university is a 'deep' goal that is likely to require extensive exploration.

A further element of the goal-setting process is exploring options for achieving the goals identified. It is the responsibility of the helper to ensure that the client considers a range of possible options that may assist in the achievement of their goals. It is easy to confuse this exploration of options with action planning, but the activities are different. For example, if we take Ashraf's wish to improve his organisational skills, there are a range of possible options open to him:

- Set aside time each day to focus on school work.
- List the tasks to be done on a daily basis.
- Prioritise the tasks to be done.
- Access an 'app' that will remind him of deadlines.
- Keep a diary.
- Ask a friend or family member to check that he is on track.
- Give up his part-time job in order to focus on his studies.

The list of possible options for improving Ashraf's organisational skills could go on. But this does not mean that all the options listed are helpful or appropriate in Ashraf's case. As in all aspects of helping, it is the client who is encouraged to identify the options available to them that relate to their goals. By using open and hypothetical questions and demonstrating the skill of challenge where appropriate, helpers can assist clients to consider options that will help them to achieve their goals. Case Study 4 in Part II provides a good example of the way in which a helper can assist their clients to consider options to achieve their goals. In Diane's case, her goal was to rebuild a relationship of trust, and a number of options to achieve this were discussed before appropriate action was agreed and taken.

Activity: Considering options to achieve goals

Return to the previous activity where you identified short-, medium- and long-term goals. Now identify a range of options for achieving these goals – what could you do to make these goals become reality? In the first instance, be as creative as you can with options for achieving goals. Once you have a full, creative and comprehensive list of options, take time to reflect and consider which options will be most realistic for you. Keep your notes, as we will come back to this activity later in the chapter when we focus on action planning.

By engaging in this activity you have paralleled the process that takes place in a helping relationship. The difference here is that you have gone through this process on your own. In helping interventions it is the role of the helper to encourage clients to identify a range of options, explore each option, reflect on each option, and come to a decision regarding which option/s will be most appropriate in relation to the goals they have set and their own personal context. It is here that helpers are likely to apply advanced skills of challenge, silence and immediacy (see Chapter 4) as well as their foundation helping skills of active listening, helpful questioning and summarising.

Action planning

Once clients have identified the goals they want to work towards and decided upon the best options to achieve those goals, then the next stage within an integrative helping model focuses on action. The point has been made consistently that helping relationships are purposeful and strive for meaning and change. Making change will require clients to take action, and often it is this final step that proves to be the most challenging. In order to support clients at this stage of the process, helpers have a significant part to play. Although it is the clients themselves who must decide on the action they would like to take in order to work towards achieving their goals, the role of the helper is key.

Culley and Bond (2011) suggest that using a brainstorming technique can be helpful in considering action steps. Table 5.1 demonstrates a brainstorming approach to action planning in practice, where Chantelle, a young single parent who is struggling with her role as mother and full-time employee, considers action steps to achieve one of her short-term goals.

Here we can see that Chantelle has identified one clear goal. She has explored a number of options for achieving that goal and has decided that there are three options which are best for her situation. With support from her helper, Chantelle identifies a number of possible action steps, as part of a brainstorming conversation, which will help her to address her options and ultimately achieve her goal. These have been evaluated by encouraging Chantelle to reflect on and discuss the pros and cons of each action step. Undertaking this force-field analysis (a term used to describe the examination of pros and cons) can be helpful at this stage in order to identify the elements that will hinder – and those that will facilitate – action. This enables Chantelle to reach a decision about which steps she feels most able to take at this time. Notice that a timescale is attached to each agreed action step. The reason for this is that we are more likely to take action if we identify a timeframe within which the action is completed. If the action is 'open-ended' we

Table 5.1 Example of action planning

The goal	Chantelle's ideas for possible options for achieving her goal	Chantelle's decision about best options	Chantelle's ideas for possible action steps to achieve each option	Chantelle decides what action to take
Spend more quality time with my children	Work fewer hours	Work fewer hours	Speak to manager Speak to colleagues about possible jobshare Look for alternative employment working fewer hours	Speak to manager, next week
	Plan time more effectively in order to fit in work and home responsibilities			
	Ask for support from family and friends			
	Talk to children about activities they would like to do together			
	Visit the local children's centre for ideas about activities that are available			
	Identify a time each day to sit and read with children	Read to children each night	Set a specific time (7pm) for reading each night	Starting from tomorrow, sit down and read with children at 7pm each night
	Identify one clear day at the weekend to spend with the children	Set a day aside each weekend to spend with the children	Choose which day at the weekend will be best Draw up a plan of the day/activities on a wall chart Invite other adults with young children to join in with some of the activities planned Ask for support from family and friends in looking after children on the 'chores day'	From next week, set aside Sunday as 'family day' Make a wall chart with children this weekend and identify possible activities they would like to do

are less likely to commit to it and achieve our goals. Reid and Fielding concur, suggesting that 'action plans need to be specific and realistic, and allow a reasonable timeframe for the achievement of action and goals' (2007: 107). As in goal setting, the SMART acronym can be applied equally to the action-planning stage of the process.

The helper – counsellor, coach or mentor – is likely to apply skills of challenge and immediacy at this stage of the process. Chapter 4 explains how the skills associated with challenge help clients to be realistic. At this point in the helping process, like the goal-setting phase where clients are planning action they will undertake, it is imperative that their action steps are achievable and realistic. It is the role of the helper to encourage clients to reflect on realism and to identify the barriers they may encounter to achieving the action they have planned.

Culley and Bond (2011) identify some key reasons as to why some clients do not take the action steps that they appear to have committed to in the helping intervention. They suggest a number of factors that prohibit clients from succeeding. Put simply these include:

- Not having the skills – clients do not have the required skills to undertake the action they have identified. So, for example, using Chantelle's action steps as identified above, if she does not have the skills or confidence to speak to her manager about reducing her working hours, then this action step will not be achieved.
- The action involves risk taking – to use the same example, there may be an element of risk in Chantelle making a case for reduced working hours to her employer. She may be anxious that her employer is going to react negatively and that her job may be in jeopardy if she makes it clear that she wants to work fewer hours.
- There are constraints – again, to use the same example, Chantelle might realise that to reduce her working hours is simply not possible because of her financial constraints.
- The rewards of taking the action are not seen as great enough – in Chantelle's case, she may perceive that the risks associated with taking the action step of talking to her employer are too great compared to the ultimate potential benefit.
- The client's need for a risk-free, perfect action plan – every action plan is likely to carry some element of risk, and therefore clients will never be able to identify the 'perfect' plan.

This highlights the importance of taking the time to evaluate each action step before it is finally agreed. I would add to this list:

- Fear of failure – some clients may seek change, whilst at the same time fearing the unknown; in these cases a number of possibilities occur:

1. No action is agreed upon or taken – clients take a 'Yes, but ...' approach to action planning.
2. Too many action points are identified – this will make it impossible to achieve everything (or anything) and the client can then comfort themselves that what they had wanted to do was impossible.
3. Action points are too ambitious or unrealistic – this means that there is no chance of action ever being achieved.

It is important to be clear that deciding not to take action is not the same as doing nothing. Clients are as active in the process of *not* taking action as they are in carrying out the actions they have agreed upon. This may sound unlikely, but it is important to be aware that clients have made decisions about *not* taking action, just as they would have made a decision if the action had been carried out.

It is crucial that helpers take a no-blame approach when working with clients who find it hard to take action in spite of their eagerness to make change. Bearing in mind the core condition of unconditional positive regard, challenging clients to think about what stopped them taking action is an important part of the helping process. Helpers should be mindful that clients may be feeling defensive, or even believe that they have let you down when they have agreed on action but not carried it out. The following questions, posed from a no-blame stance, can be useful in challenging clients sensitively and positively: 'I wonder what got in the way of your doing what you had planned?', or 'What could you do differently to ensure that you are able to take these steps next time?', or 'I'm wondering if we need to go back and review the action that you have set yourself. What do you think?'

Activity: Identifying action steps

I want you to go back to your list of options for achieving goals noted down in the previous activity. Select one of the options you identified and brainstorm a list of possible action steps that you could take in order to address this option and work towards achieving your goal. Using a force-field-analysis approach, reflect on the pros and cons of each possible action step. Now decide upon the most appropriate action steps for you and ensure that they are SMART (specific, measurable, achievable, realistic, time-bound).

I suspect that this activity took some time to complete. This is because the process is complex and requires practice. It is also likely that you did this on your own, without discussing your thoughts with another person. The beauty of helping is that another interested, engaged, non-judgemental and empathic person is committed to supporting and challenging this process to ensure that appropriate action steps are identified, evaluated and carried out.

Each of the case studies outlined in Part II demonstrates, to a greater or lesser extent, what actions have been taken and which goals have been achieved by clients in the range of settings illustrated.

Summary

The focus of this chapter is on key processes that form an integral part of helping: contracting at the outset of helping, agreeing an agenda for each session, goal setting, and action planning. The skills of active listening, helpful questioning, summarising and reflecting back are used throughout the process, and the advanced skills allied to challenge, immediacy and silence are applied particularly in the goal-setting and action-planning phase. The advanced skill of information sharing will be used early on when the contract is agreed. Finally, the point should be reinforced once again that helping is not a linear process. What is set out here – in terms of a chronology that describes the helping process – is useful, but it should not be viewed as either mechanistic or inflexible. The joy of working in the helping professions is that we are dealing with human beings who, by their very nature, are complex. Often, when they seek help, clients are in crisis or chaos. It is important that, throughout, the helper keeps the 'goals of helping' in mind and attends to the process of helping flexibly – sensitive at all times to the client's needs.

Further reading suggestions

Cameron, H. (2008) *The Counselling Interview: A Guide for the Helping Professions.* Basingstoke: Palgrave Macmillan – Part 1 of this book examines the helping process, whilst Part 6 focuses on goal setting; a useful and practical read.

Reid, H.L. and Fielding, A.J. (2007) *Providing Support to Young People: A Guide to Interviewing in Helping Relationships.* Oxon: Routledge – Although this book focuses on helping relationships with young people, it offers an excellent overview of the process and skills applied in any helping context.

van Nieuwerburgh, C. (2014) *An Introduction to Coaching Skills: A Practical Guide.* London: Sage – Parts two and three of this accessible text focus on skills and processes in the coaching context.

6

THE REFLECTIVE AND REFLEXIVE HELPER

BARBARA BASSOT

Chapter objectives: Readers will have the opportunity to ...

- define the terms 'reflective', 'critically reflective' and 'reflexive practice';
- develop self-awareness by engaging with a range of activities through the chapter;
- identify how reflection and reflexivity are central to counselling, coaching and mentoring;
- consider the application of a range of reflective practice models.

Introduction

This chapter explores the vital nature of reflective practice and reflexivity within counselling, coaching and mentoring. Many practitioners seek to take a thoughtful approach to their practice, and having an understanding of the place and purpose of critical reflection is essential for effective helping relationships. The chapter begins with an examination of some key terms and seeks to eliminate some potential confusion between them. It goes on to explore some of the reasons for their importance in professional practice. Some useful theoretical models are then discussed, followed by practical activities that help you to apply them to your work and studies. This is followed by some helpful tips for embedding reflection into your work and life, highlighting the vital aspect of making time to reflect in our busy, everyday lives. The chapter concludes with some final thoughts and suggestions for further reading.

Defining key terms

Unfortunately, in published literature, terms related to reflection are not necessarily defined clearly; in addition, the words 'reflection', 'reflectivity' and 'reflexivity' are sometimes used interchangeably, which can be very confusing. So, what is reflection? If you were to look in a concise English dictionary for a definition of the word 'reflection', you would find at least two things: the first is a noun that relates to mirror images, and the second a verb – 'to think deeply'. This gives us very helpful clues regarding the nature of reflective practice and what it involves. Put simply, it is rather like looking in a mirror to see ourselves and our work more clearly, and then giving some careful thought to what we see.

Reflectivity is often defined as the deliberate act of reflection. This chimes with Kolb's (1984) experiential learning cycle, where he suggests that we learn by having an experience that we then reflect on afterwards. This is often done intentionally, particularly when we are learning a new skill or are on some kind of programme of study or professional development. Schön (1983) calls this reflection-on-action, where a practitioner spends some time thinking through what they have done after the event. In addition, Schön also discusses the concept of reflection-*in*-action, where professionals are able to think about things as they are doing something else; he calls this 'thinking on your feet'. So, a counsellor, coach or mentor is able to interact with a client and to think about what they are doing at the same time, for example discussing an issue with a client and thinking about how the client is responding.

In more recent years some writers have begun to use the term 'critically reflective practice' (Thompson and Thompson, 2008), which suggests that it is not enough simply to reflect on our experience, but that we need to take a critical approach to it too. However, this does not mean that we only focus on negative aspects, but are open to seeing the positives as well. Here we formulate a critique of our practice as we question it, remembering not to fall prey to deficit models that only focus on negatives.

Reflexivity takes the concept of critically reflective practice several steps further. As a term it has the potential to be confusing: we might initially assume that reflexivity is about our reflex actions or those things that we tend to do automatically. In some senses this is correct, but it involves being aware of the things we do automatically (for example, the assumptions we make) and then questioning them so that we can challenge them when and where appropriate. This means that we avoid seeing only what we expect to see. In addition reflexivity makes us aware of our professional context and any issues of power that might be evident in relationships and organisations; this enables us to work in an anti-discriminatory way (Fook and Askeland, 2006).

In relation to working with clients in the context of counselling, coaching and mentoring, we need to be mindful that issues of power will often be present in interpersonal relationships and that clients usually feel that the power lies with the professional practitioner and not with them; we continually need to remember to work hard at developing a relationship of equals.

Critically reflective practice and reflexivity then involve a process of becoming more self-aware. Many of the students I work with have said things like, 'I knew I would learn a lot on my course, but I never realised how much I would learn about myself'. A high level of self-awareness means that I understand myself in relation to a range of important issues. Some of these are as follows.

- Strengths
- Weaknesses or areas for development
- Attitudes
- Personal and professional values
- Prejudices
- Assumptions
- How I come across to other people
- 'Triggers', for example the things that are likely to upset or annoy me
- Feelings

Activity: Self-awareness

Think about the list above and write some notes under each of the points regarding how you understand yourself at the moment. Are there any other points you would like to add?

Critical reflection and reflexivity are vital for professional practice in the field of counselling, coaching and mentoring for the following reasons:

- In order to ensure that helpers are meeting ethical standards, guidelines and legal requirements.
- *Gaining self-awareness* – as discussed above, being a reflexive practitioner means that we are aware of our attitudes and values and the impact they have on our work. This awareness means that we are able to make choices when needed. For example, we can stand

back from our attitudes and values, disclose them to the client where appropriate or, in exceptional circumstances, refer the client to another practitioner who is better placed to offer support than we are. This means that we are in a stronger position to practise ethically, keeping the client at the centre of the process.

- *Being aware of feelings* – reflecting on our emotional responses to situations can be a very helpful guide to gaining a deeper under-standing of our practice. Our feelings can act as a guide to our practice, particularly when we find ourselves experiencing some kind of inner discomfort.
- *Being aware of assumptions* – reflexive practitioners are slow to make assumptions; critical reflection helps us to question the things we take for granted and prevents us from accepting things at face value. It also enables us to be curious about our practice.
- *Evaluating practice* – being a professional means that we need to continually examine our practice in order to keep our knowledge and skills up to date. Reflection aids professional learning and gives us a means of constructing professional knowledge – all profes-sional practitioners build up a wealth of knowledge over time.
- *Making practice creative* – this means we are open to trying out new ideas and methods so that our work continually develops.
- *Preventing stagnation* – reflecting on practice means that we are sure to keep our focus on the client and their needs. This means that our practice does not become stale or repetitive, but remains fresh.
- *Only being satisfied with excellence* – many professions use the language of competence, which can be described as some kind of baseline where practitioners are seen to be good enough. Critical reflection keeps us 'on our toes' and striving for excellence for the benefit of our clients.
- *Making practice creative* – this means we are open to trying out new ideas and methods so that our work moves forward.
- *Providing an aid for supervision* – reflection encourages us to exam-ine things that surprise us and disturb us in the safe space that supervision provides.
- *Preventing burn-out* – the personal and professional demands of counselling, coaching and mentoring are many, and reflection helps us to take time out to examine how we are coping and to take appropriate action if and when necessary.

Activity: The importance of critical reflection

Think about the list above and write some notes under each of them. Are there any that seem to be particularly important for you at the moment?

Some useful theoretical models

There are several useful models of reflection, and many of them can be put into one of the following three categories.

1. *Cyclical models* – these models speak of cycles of reflection with steps or stages that follow in sequence. Many of these models (but not all) are based on the work of Kolb (1984), in particular his experiential learning cycle discussed above. These models are often helpful as they give us a starting point and help us to build a habit of reflection. It is important to remember that any model asserting that certain things happen in a certain order will be open to critique, particularly the question, 'Does it always happen in that particular order?' The response to this will invariably be 'No', or 'It depends'. Other examples of cyclical models are Driscoll's (2007) 'What?' model (drawn from Borton's Developmental Framework (1970)) and Gibbs' (1998) reflective cycle.
2. *Structured models* – these models seek to break down aspects of reflection, often by posing questions. They can help us to examine our practice in more detail by reminding us to consider our feelings and assumptions and the context in which we practise. Any model that tries to categorise critical reflection will also be open to critique on the grounds of whether or not the questions posed are always appropriate in a particular situation. An example of this is Johns' (2004) structured model of reflection, which he has developed and modified over a number of years.
3. *Hierarchical models* – these models often describe reflection operating at different levels and, as our work and study progress, they help us to see how we can think about our practice more and more deeply. They can help us to develop our skills of reflection by showing us how to move from thinking about our practice generally in order to evaluate it (reflection), through to deliberately reflecting on aspects of ourselves and our practice, often in response to critical incidents (reflectivity), and then to a critical examination of our attitudes, values and assumptions (reflexivity). Such models are also open to critique because it is arguable whether reflection can be broken down in such a specific way. Examples of structured models are Mezirow's (1981) seven levels of reflectivity and Johns' (2013) typology of reflection.

We will now examine four different models of reflection: Ghaye's cyclical model, Johns' five levels of reflection, Mezirow's seven levels of reflectivity, and Bassot's integrated reflective cycle.

A cyclical model of reflection – Ghaye

In contrast with many reflective models that focus on difficulties and problems, Ghaye's (2011) model is written from the perspective of positive psychology and appreciative enquiry, and emphasises that we need to focus on positive experiences. This can help to motivate us and encourage us to build on what is working well.

Ghaye (2011: 2) describes his reflective approach as 'strengths-based' and he puts forward six key ideas in relation to reflection:

1. Links with practice – reflection can motivate us and help us to develop new ideas for high-quality work;
2. Emotions – reflection asks us to examine our emotional response to experiences and situations;
3. Often structured – this can help our thought processes, especially when we are new to reflection;
4. Often involves looking back on past experiences – but we should also consider what is happening in the present and look to the future;
5. Helps us to see what we are good at – we can then see what we can achieve and how we can develop;
6. Can be triggered by many different things – posing questions about our practice helps us to examine it critically.

As well as reflection-on-action and reflection-in-action, Ghaye also discusses two other types of reflection:

- Reflection-*for*-action – this he describes as fundamental. Such reflection is done for a particular reason, for example because we want to understand something better, to develop something, or to improve it. This is often done as part of a process of planning how to address a specific issue.
- Reflection-*with*-action – the focus here is on the future, and it is thinking that leads to action. This could include things you might do as an individual or with others as part of a team.

Ghaye's strengths-based model encourages us to build on positives by asking the following questions.

- What is working well right now? (*Appreciate*)
- What do we need to change to make things better? (*Imagine*)
- How can we achieve this? (*Design*)
- Who needs to take action and what will the consequences be? (*Act*)

This model is represented diagrammatically with the four points above located in sequence on a capital letter R, which represents 'reflection'.

Activity: Ghaye's model

Think about an experience you have had recently and write some notes under each of the four questions above. How does this help you focus on the positives of the experience?

A structured model of reflection – Johns

Working in the field of nurse education, Johns (1994) devised a structured model of reflection to help students and practitioners examine their practice more deeply by posing questions. The model has the following four key aspects.

1. *Description* – first he asks us to write a description of the experience and to identify the key issues within our record of the experience that we need to pay attention to.
2. *Reflection* – here he asks us to consider what we were trying to achieve, why we acted as we did, and what the consequences of our actions were for ourselves, our colleagues and our clients. He also asks us to examine our feelings and those of the client during the experience. Regarding the latter, he asks us to consider how we knew what the client felt (for example, from what they said or from their body language).
3. *Any influencing factors* – Johns encourages us here to think about the context of the experience, including both the internal and external factors that might have influenced us and whether there were any sources of knowledge that could or should have influenced what we did. This helps us to assess our options, for example whether there were any alternative strategies we could have taken to deal with the situation better and what the consequences of these might have been.
4. *Learning* – here he poses questions around what sense we can make of this experience now and for the future, how we feel about it, and what action we can take to support ourselves and those around us. Importantly he asks how this experience has changed our way of knowing in practice.

Activity: Johns' model

Now think of an experience you have had recently (it could be the same as the one above or something different) and again write some notes under each of the four headings above. How does this help you to reflect on your experience? How does this compare to the previous activity you did?

A hierarchical model of reflection – Mezirow

Hierarchical models of reflection help us to examine how we approach people and situations – in particular any assumptions we might be making based on our past experiences. One such model is that of Mezirow (1978; 1981), which describes seven levels of reflectivity. The first four levels relate to things that we are generally aware of as they form part of our ordinary consciousness (OC); they include an examination of our feelings and values. The other three levels lie outside our general awareness and are held within the realm of our critical consciousness (CC); these can be discovered through critical reflection, and include the reasons why we do certain things and act in particular ways. Here our assumptions come into play, and the reasons why we might be quick to make judgements about people and situations can become clearer. The seven levels are as follows.

1. *Reflectivity (OC)* – becoming aware of our perceptions, for example how we see things and how we think and act.
2. *Affective Reflectivity (OC)* – we become more aware of our feelings about our perceptions.
3. *Discriminant Reflectivity (OC)* – we begin to question whether or not our perceptions about people and situations are accurate.
4. *Judgemental Reflectivity (OC)* – makes us aware of any value judgements we might be making and takes us into the realm of beginning to consider our assumptions.
5. *Conceptual Reflectivity (CC)* – helps us both to question the ways in which we think about other people and to consider whether our assumptions are accurate and justifiable.
6. *Psychic Reflectivity (CC)* – takes us into the realm of recognising our own prejudices which can cause us to make quick judgements about people with insufficient evidence; this means we begin to recognise if we are jumping to conclusions.
7. *Theoretical Reflectivity (CC)* – we begin to see that the roots of our quick judgements are cultural and psychological.

It is clear that this structural model, although complex, is useful in helping us to examine our practice at a much deeper level. It is interesting to note that Mezirow uses the term 'reflectivity' throughout; looking back at our earlier definitions, it appears that levels 4–7 above take us into the realm of reflexivity, where we analyse our practice by examining our feelings, assumptions and values. Whilst this might not be a model that we use every day, it could be helpful when considering issues that are particularly challenging. Examining our thinking at each level means that we turn off any kind of 'autopilot', set aside things that we take for granted, and question our assumptions. As a result we are in a better position to challenge our assumptions, and reframe them when we feel they are not justifiable. Mezirow argues that assumptions are always influenced by culture and that by reaching the deepest level – theoretical reflectivity – transformation of perspective can happen; in other words, we can begin to think about things differently.

Activity: Mezirow's seven levels of reflectivity

Now think of an experience that it would be useful to analyse using Mezirow's model. Which of the levels were you able to use? How did it help you to challenge your assumptions and values? How might it help you to develop reflexivity?

Bassot's integrated reflective cycle

My own model – the integrated reflective cycle (Bassot, 2013) – is shown below; it draws on some key reflective practice literature. It is always useful to compare and contrast different theoretical approaches, as this can help you to find the ones that you find most helpful. In addition you might incorporate particular aspects of models as part of your own reflective processes.

Taking a questioning approach to professional practice is an excellent way of examining our practice at a deeper level. The integrated reflective cycle is not completely new and, like many others, draws on the work of Kolb (1984). It also uses some of the questions posed by Gibbs (1998) and Johns (2004).

The cycle begins with an experience: we are encouraged to describe what happened but also to think about the context of the experience. The context of an experience can have a major impact on how we view

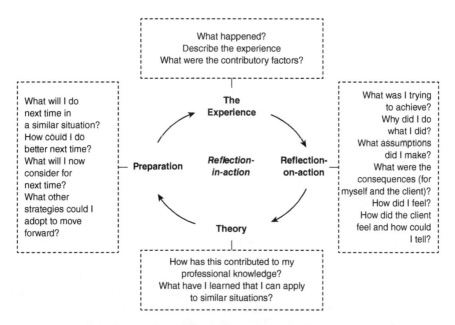

Figure 6.1   Bassot's integrated reflective cycle

Source: Bassot, B. (2016) *The Reflective Practice Guide*. Abingdon: Routledge. p. 145.

it, to the point where we might act differently in a similar situation in a different context. The cycle also asks us to examine the contributory factors, some of which might stem from the past (memories of our previous experiences, for example) and the present (for example the practice environment).

We are then asked to reflect-on-action (Schön, 1983) in order to critique our approach. This includes an examination of our feelings and any assumptions we might be making. In addition we are asked to think about the possible consequences of our feelings and assumptions, and to imagine how the client might have experienced things too.

We are then asked to examine how this experience can contribute to our professional knowledge, for example what we can learn that we could later apply to other similar situations. We can focus on both what is new that we can add to what we already know and anything that is different that we need to pay some attention to.

The final step on the cycle asks us to look forward to see how this knowledge and experience might be used in the future. Here it is important to consider any helpful strategies that we could adopt next time.

Reflection-in-action is shown in the centre of the cycle; this highlights the notion that this kind of 'thinking on our feet' happens all the time and needs to be done throughout any experience.

Developing the skill of reflection

If reflection is not something that comes easily to you, it is easy to fall into the trap of thinking of it as something you are not very good at. I have met people who say things like 'But I think all the time, so how is this kind of thinking any different?' It is important to remember that reflection is a skill and, like any other skill, it is not something we are born with, and – most importantly – we can all get better at it. Here are some examples of how you can develop the skill of reflection.

- *Reflective writing* – many writers (myself included) recommend the use of a journal or diary as an aid to reflection. Writing by hand slows us down (this is particularly important in our busy professional lives) and makes us focus on what we are thinking about; it is almost impossible to write something by hand while thinking about something else. Writing aids our concentration but also acts as an important means of psychological externalisation: writing about something that is troubling us means that we get it out of our heads and onto paper. This makes writing therapeutic as well as professionally developmental, and it is something that you might use in the future with some of your clients.
- *Reflective discussion* – reflection should not just be a solitary activity, and is something that we can do with others with great mutual benefit. This could mean finding a 'critical friend', a triad or a small group. In all circumstances it is important that the people concerned demonstrate the core conditions, so you can be open and honest with one another.
- *Reflecting using technology* – many of us love technology and take our smartphones and tablets with us everywhere. We can use these as tools for reflection to help us capture things that we come across. Some examples include: camera (taking photographs of things that strike us, from a beautiful sunset to a key slide from an interesting PowerPoint presentation); notepad (to remind us of things we do not want to forget); books (to download key papers or chapters that we think could help us to reflect); and podcasts (key things that we want to listen to at a later date).
- *Reflecting creatively* – some of us love being creative, and using our artistic flair can help us to reflect. This could include drawing, painting, collage, model making, sewing and tapestry. But remember that even if you do not consider yourself to be artistic, drawing diagrams or mind maps can nevertheless help us to illustrate our thoughts.
- *Finding a reflective space* – reflection is a choice, and finding a physical space for it can help us, particularly when we find it difficult

to 'switch off' from work and study. Many people like a quiet space such as a room at home or in the library where you can relax and not be distracted. Others prefer some noise around them, such as in a coffee shop. In relation to this, it is important to recognise what suits you best.

Case study: Jake (counselling, coaching and mentoring student)

Jake is studying for a degree in counselling, coaching and mentoring and understands that he needs to develop his skills of reflection. Jake is a very enthusiastic and positive person who recognises that he has a tendency to rush into situations without thinking about things first. As a result he often finds that he jumps to conclusions and then regrets speaking and acting too quickly. His tutor has asked him to consider how he can take a more measured and thoughtful approach, particularly in role-play activities. After reading a key text on critical reflection, Jake decides to set aside some time to examine his participation in role-play activities to try to understand more about why he is so quick to respond. When he explores his feelings about role play, he realises that he is often very nervous, usually because he does not want to appear foolish in front of his fellow students. In particular he is anxious about silence, which tempts him to 'jump in' rather than listening. As he has built up a good relationship with them, Jake decides to discuss this in his triad, and discovers that he is not the only one who gets nervous in such situations. Together they discuss strategies to help them to conquer their nerves.

Making time for reflection

Whether we are working or studying, many of us feel that everyday life is extremely busy and moves at a very fast pace. It is easy to slip into thinking that we do not have time to reflect, and for most of us this might well be an accurate assessment. My own view is that in my busy life I do not actually have any time, so the only time I have is the time I make. It is fair to say that if something is important to us, we will generally make time for it. When we feel we are not able to make time for the things that matter to us, we can become discouraged, even dismayed, and feel that our lives are out of balance.

Reflection offers many benefits, such as helping us to process our feelings, managing stress and coping with the many demands of professional practice. Setting aside a small amount of time each week for reflection (for example, 15 minutes twice per week) can help us in all of these areas. However, expecting to be able to slot this into our busy lives 'as and when' is unrealistic for many, and we can soon find ourselves in the position where several weeks have passed and we have not spent any time reflecting. Having a simple system in place (for example blocking out time in our diary, setting a reminder on our phone, or simply whatever works for us) will help us to prioritise this important activity.

Some final thoughts

It is clear that the benefits of reflection are many, not only for ourselves but for our clients too. Critical reflection is vital for professional learning and development because it helps us to be mindful practitioners who process their feelings, challenge their assumptions, and are not satisfied with accepting things at face value. Reflexive practitioners are curious practitioners who have the needs of their clients at the forefront of their minds, as they strive for excellence in their client-centred practice. Each of the case studies in Part II demonstrates the helper's ability to reflect on their practice with clients. They do not simply explain *what* happened in their work with each client, but seek to analyse *why* and *how* the relationship developed and the client made progress.

Further reading suggestions

Many books on reflective practice are written for people in specific professions. It is always valuable to read things that are written for your own field and here you should follow the advice of your tutors. It is also helpful to read from other professional areas too; many counsellors, coaches and mentors will have contact with others in the helping professions (for example nurses and social workers), and having some understanding of their approaches to the whole area of reflection will also be helpful. Some texts are written generically for a wide readership. Here are some suggestions.

Generic texts

Bassot, B. (2013) *The Reflective Journal.* Basingstoke: Palgrave Macmillan – If you are asked to keep a reflective journal as part of your studies, this provides a valuable source of help and support.

Bassot, B. (2016) *The Reflective Practice Guide.* Abingdon: Routledge – This gives a comprehensive consideration of a range of topics related to reflection and reflexivity.

Bolton, G. (2014) *Reflective Practice: Writing and Professional Development* (4th edn). London: Sage – If you want to develop your reflective writing skills further, this book could inspire you.

Texts written for counsellors, coaches and mentors

Bager-Charleson, S. (2010) *Reflective Practice in Counselling and Psychotherapy*. Exeter: Learning Matters – This is an accessible text that conveys complex concepts clearly.

Hay, J. (2007) *Reflective Practice and Supervision for Coaches*. Maidenhead: Open University Press – Written from the perspective of transactional analysis, this book offers lots of practical tips for reflection.

Texts written for social workers but with a very generic approach

Thompson, S. and Thompson, P. (2008) *The Critically Reflective Practitioner*. Basingstoke: Palgrave Macmillan – This book offers some excellent strategies for critical reflection and is written for people who are working with clients who face challenging situations.

Barbara Bassot

Barbara Bassot is a Senior Lecturer in Education in the Centre for Career and Personal Development, at Canterbury Christ Church University where her specialism is critically reflective practice. She is a qualified careers professional and has a Doctorate in Education.

7

THE ETHICAL DIMENSION OF HELPING

Chapter objectives: Readers will have the opportunity to ...

- define the term 'ethics';
- consider how the concept of ethical practice applies to counselling, coaching and mentoring;
- identify the principles underpinning ethical codes of practice;
- reflect on their own values, beliefs and behaviours in relation to ethical practice with clients.

Introduction

The concept of ethics is complex and requires careful unpicking and significant personal reflection on the part of the practitioner when applied to counselling, coaching and mentoring. Ethical practice is a central element to all professional helping relationships. Those who work in the helping professions should develop a sound understanding of what working ethically with clients means in theoretical terms and, more importantly, they should reflect on and demonstrate how ethical principles are adhered to throughout their practice.

Working ethically means doing what is 'right'. But the simplicity of that statement belies the depth and complexity of ethics as a philosophical concept, as 'rights' and 'truths' are not universally held assumptions, but rather are informed by a range of factors – most importantly, culture. When applied to counselling, coaching and mentoring practice, ethical decision making on the part of the helper is rarely straightforward, even when informed by ethical codes of practice. Human beings, our clients, their lives and their actions are often 'messy'. There is always the potential for conflict and tension between what we and our clients consider to be right or wrong regarding how we act, what we believe, and what we think is significant.

This chapter begins by defining the term 'ethics'. It establishes the concepts of ethics, morals and values and strives to make a meaningful distinction between each, whilst recognising the common ground shared by these concepts. It goes on to explore the importance of ethics in counselling, coaching and mentoring, drawing on professional ethical codes of practice. Throughout, you will be asked to consider the concept of ethics and ethical working in your current or future work context. This will often mean asking yourself challenging and searching questions. Because ethics deals with what is 'right', there has to be an underlying assumption that there is also a 'wrong'. There may be some truth in the assertion that certain behaviours and responses might be considered wrong, damaging or inappropriate (universally). But one person's 'wrong' may not be shared by another, or our rights and wrongs may alter depending upon the context. We might agree, for example, that to use violence against a fellow human being is wrong, but if protecting a loved one who is at risk, would we still stand by that belief? Some people might argue 'yes', whilst others may feel less sure, as our personal and emotional responses inform our judgements. There are significant links between this chapter and the preceding chapter on reflective practice, whereby developing reflexivity requires an ability to understand 'difference' and to be aware of the impact of our own moral and ethical codes and responses in relation to others.

There are no universally agreed principles about what constitutes right and wrong which are accepted and adhered to across different cultures and societies. Therefore each individual must make their own judgements and be able to justify their decisions and actions. These judgements and actions are informed, in the professional context, by the guiding principles set out in an ethical code of practice.

Before proceeding further, it is important to sound a small note of caution here by emphasising that this chapter serves as an *introduction* to the subject of ethics. It is important to note that, unlike other, more practical chapters in this book, the concepts explored here are philosophical in nature and can be tricky to engage with, explain and understand fully in the space available. This chapter offers some broad principles but, like ethics itself, it cannot provide every answer or offer definitive solutions. The professional judgement of the helper is paramount; this judgement is informed by the practitioner's personal values which underpin firmly held beliefs, developed as a result of life experiences and background. As already suggested, every helper must use their professional judgement, develop their reflexivity through supervision, and work alongside their profession's code of practice to ensure professional decision making and integrity in their work with their clients, even in the 'greyest' of areas. Further reading is suggested at the end of the chapter for those who want to delve more deeply into this fascinating dimension of helping practice.

Ethics – a definition

Unsurprisingly there are a number of definitions of ethics and ethical practice in the counselling, coaching and mentoring literature. Most make the link between morals, values and ethics, and many use the terms 'morals' and 'ethics' interchangeably (Banks, 2001). This is not as strange as it may appear, as one of the terms derives from Greek and one from Roman sources, but both when translated share the same definition: doing what is right. Some people contest the shared meaning of the terms (Osborne, 1998), but many interpret morals and ethics as meaning the same thing and, as suggested, both words are often used with no obvious distinction in the literature. It might be helpful to clarify by identifying *morals* as our own internal beliefs about what is right or wrong, whereas our *ethical* practice is informed by our profession's code of practice. Ethical practice is a prevailing scheme of morals and values and this may, at times, differ from our own moral judgements about particular issues. McLeod (1998) confirms that our morals and values – deeply held beliefs about what is right and wrong, good and bad – should be guided by an ethical code in order to ensure that we work with the client's goals in mind, rather than our own. As suggested above, at times our own and our client's morals may be in conflict, but as McLeod explains:

> In general, most counsellors would agree that the aim of counselling is to help people arrive at what is right for them, rather than attempting to impose a solution from outside ... The dilemma for the counsellor is to allow herself to be powerful and influential without imposing her own moral values and choices. Good counsellors, therefore, need to possess an informed awareness of the different ways in which moral and ethical issues may arise in their work. (1998: 264)

He goes on to explain that those in helping relationships will be aware of their professional code of ethics, which will inform their response when their own and their clients' moral judgements are in conflict or where 'grey areas' emerge.

Activity: Defining ethics

Before we explore some of the definitions of ethics in the literature, take a moment to complete the sentence below, coming up with your own definition of morals and ethical working:

'A definition of morals is ......

and working ethically means ......'

My own response to this activity might be:

A definition of morals is my own deeply held beliefs about what is right and wrong, good and bad, influenced by my culture, religion, background, upbringing and my life's experiences; and working ethically means that I ensure at all times that I work in the best interest of the client, whilst being mindful of the ethical codes that inform my practice.

My suggestion here supports what McLeod asserts earlier – that my own morals and values may, at times, be in conflict with what is best for the client. For example, I might believe in a woman's right to make decisions about her own future, in relation to her career, her choice of partner, and so on. I may be working with a female client who holds a very different moral standpoint, based on her own beliefs and her social and cultural value systems, and relies on her husband for advice, handing over responsibility for her life to her partner. At times like these, my ethical code of practice provides me with a set of guiding principles which I can consult and reflect upon when situations are not clear-cut and I hold different moral principles to my clients.

The following case study offers an example of a situation where a school counsellor's own morals were challenged by her client, presenting her with an ethical dilemma.

Case study: Personal morals and ethical practice

Chloe is a counsellor in a school. She has been working intensively in a helping relationship with Theo, a young man of 16 who is heavily involved with a violent gang in his local area. Theo's attendance at school is erratic and his engagement with learning is minimal, but is improving. Recently, Theo has intimated that he is having a sexual relationship with a 13-year-old in the school. In addition, he has also disclosed to Chloe his involvement

(Continued)

(Continued)

in other violent and illegal activities outside of school. Chloe is uncertain about what she should do. She is a Catholic with firm beliefs regarding sexual relationships, although she knows that her own beliefs and those of her clients will often be in conflict. She has a confidential relationship with Theo (whereby only issues of 'significant harm' can be disclosed to the school), yet Chloe is aware that Theo is breaking the law and putting himself, and possibly others, in danger. Chloe has also invested much time and energy into building a relationship of trust with Theo, and she feels that the counselling is beginning to help Theo to understand himself better and to make more informed decisions about his life. She knows that this relationship is fragile and she does not want to risk damaging it by breaking confidentiality and trust.

This case study highlights the tensions inherent in working ethically. Chloe will need to reflect in depth before she makes her decision about whether to break confidentiality or not. We will revisit this case study in a moment. First, let us try to untangle the complexity of ethics further and consider its application in helping relationships. Cox, Bachkirova and Clutterbuck suggest that:

> where the very act of engagement has emotional and moral ramifications, it is more necessary and more difficult to describe correct ethical behaviour. It is in precisely this zone of subtle moral judgement that the most important dimension of an ethical practice lies. (2014: 434)

Tim Bond (2015) has written widely on ethics, particularly in relation to the counselling profession. He has also been heavily involved in reviewing and revising the BACP's ethical code of practice. His definition of ethics noted here is accessible and straightforward: 'Ethics provide ideas and terminology for considering what is morally good or bad and how to distinguish good from bad' (p. 8). He goes on to emphasise the importance of ethics in counselling practice:

> Counselling depends on clients being able to trust their counsellors. They trust their feelings of vulnerability to someone who is committed to using their knowledge and skills to act in the best interests of their clients. Professions honour and respect this trust by setting standards for their practitioners and expecting them to act ethically. Good standards and ethical practice provide the best possible conditions for clients to discuss freely whatever is causing them concern and for the counsellor to work therapeutically. (2015: 7)

Haynes (1998) makes a helpful point that ethics is central to anyone who asks themselves the questions 'What ought I to do?' or 'Would this decision and action be right?' in their professional role. This includes those in the helping professions.

Activity: What would you do?

Return to the previous case study where Chloe is concerned about breaking confidentiality with Theo. Note down your thoughts on what action you would take in this situation. Who might you go to for support?

In the first instance, Chloe must take this case to supervision. Supervision provides the opportunity for Chloe to reflect on the issues that she is facing, whilst gaining an experienced and objective perspective from her supervisor. If necessary, Chloe and her supervisor can revisit the ethical code of practice in order to clarify precisely some key terms; for example, what is meant by 'significant harm' and does it apply in this case? And what are Chloe's legal responsibilities if her client has admitted a sexual relationship with a young person who is 'under age', and has disclosed involvement in 'illegal activity'? Whatever the outcome, Chloe has a continuing responsibility to Theo. She must ensure that she discusses any actions which she is required to take with her client so that he is aware of what the outcomes are likely to be; and, if possible, she can continue to support him. It is also worth referring to Case Study 8 in Part II, where Joe is being supported by a trainee probation officer, Sally. She describes a disruption in the helping relationship because Joe reoffends and the decision is made at a senior level to return him to custody. Sally is concerned about this decision and its long-term impact on the helping relationship and the work with Joe.

To summarise thus far, knowledge of ethics and adherence to ethical practice is central to the work of anyone who is engaging in helping relationships. Recognising that our 'rights' and 'wrongs' may be different to our clients' is imperative. We will ask ourselves many times over the course of our helping practice: 'What should I do now?' and 'What is the right thing to do in this case?' We should also remind ourselves that these decisions are not made in isolation. Regular support and supervision should be in place to enable us to reflect and reach an appropriate decision in each tricky case (see Chapter 9). We will also have access to our professional ethical code to guide us. As already explained and demonstrated in this chapter, the nature of the work, focused as it is on the human condition, is often messy and rarely clear-cut. Every professional helper will ask themselves, at regular points in their work, whether or not they are making the right decision and taking appropriate action – this is reflective practice. But it is likely that two counsellors, coaches and mentors in the same situation might arrive at different conclusions and take different actions; and it is likely that neither is 'wrong'. This is what makes the work so fascinating.

Activity: Ethical challenges

It might help to undertake this activity with someone else, perhaps an experienced helper. Begin by listing a range of situations or scenarios that you can envisage with clients which might present you with an ethical challenge. Reflect on the situations you have identified. What are the common themes or factors that would be particularly challenging for you to work with? What makes these particular themes/factors challenging for you? Think about your values and beliefs.

Every individual who completes this activity will identify different personal challenges relating to ethical practice. There are no 'rights' and 'wrongs'. The important thing in the helping professions is to be aware of the times and situations when we feel challenged, and to reflect on what these challenges are and where they come from in relation to our own beliefs, values and knowledge of ethical practice. Together, these elements are often referred to as our 'moral compass'.

Ethical practice – the principles

Medicine is a profession where some of the earliest debates about ethical practice emerged. Decisions about treatments that may have serious consequences for the patient have always been central to medical practice. The Hippocratic oath is a good example of a set of ethical standards and principles that medical practitioners still 'sign up to' today. Beauchamp and Childress (2008) identify four key principles in medical ethics. These are:

- respect – for the rights and autonomy of individuals;
- beneficence – a commitment to doing what is of benefit to clients;
- non-maleficence – a commitment to avoiding harm to clients;
- justice – an approach to distributing services fairly.

At first glance these principles appear fair and reasonable and embrace what we would all aspire to in our work with clients. That said, adhering to these principles is not always straightforward. There are on-going and significant debates in medicine today that call these principles into question. For example, the current discussion regarding euthanasia demonstrates conflict between these principles. Both 'respect' (for the right of individuals to make decisions about their lives) and 'benefi-cence' (doing what the client believes is best) could be seen to conflict with 'non-maleficence' (commitment to avoiding harm to the individual). However, it could be argued that harm is being done by not allowing people to die when they believe their lives are not worth living. Ethical dilemmas are called as such because they involve professionals making decisions which may at times conflict with an individual ethical principle.

The four principles outlined above have come to form the bedrock of what is regarded as ethical practice in a range of helping professions. Banks (2012) adapts the wording of these four principles when she writes from a social work perspective. She suggests the following:

1. Respect for and promotion of each individual's rights to their own decision making.
2. Promotion of welfare or well-being of the individual.
3. Equality for client practice.
4. Distributive justice.

Thompson (1990), writing from a psychotherapeutic perspective, adds two further principles for ethical practice in the counselling context:

*   *Fidelity* – ensuring that trust between client and counsellor is not broken.
*   *Self-interest* – the right of the counsellor to hold these ethical principles as part of practice.

The points below summarise the ethical principles detailed above, and assist us to reflect on what these mean in helping practice. In brief, those who work in the helping professions engage with these principles in the following way:

*   They value each client as an individual and respect every client's right to hold their own values and beliefs. Furthermore they believe that it is the *client* who is responsible for making decisions and taking actions with regard to their own lives. It is not the role of the helper to impose their own views or wishes based on their own set of values and beliefs, which may be at odds with their client.

- They are committed to working in the best interest of each client, ensuring that their client's well-being is central and paramount. This means demonstrating care and empathy, whilst enabling clients to identify ways in which they can improve their state of emotional and psychological well-being.
- They do not do anything that could potentially harm the client during the helping process. In the helping context, 'harm' refers to emotional and psychological harm; whereas challenge is central to helping practice, criticism of the client is certainly not, and abuse of the relationship between helper and client can be potentially damaging.
- They are committed to fairness and equality in their practice, whilst recognising and acknowledging the diverse and unique individual needs of clients. Fairness and equality do not mean treating everyone in the same way (see Chapter 8), but rather recognising the uniqueness of each client and responding to their needs appropriately.
- They ensure that a relationship of trust is maintained throughout. In the helping context this particularly relates to issues of confidentiality. Helpers need to be clear about the boundaries of the relationship and ensure that these boundaries are adhered to.
- They recognise that the helping relationship is unique and different from other relationships they have in their lives: friends, family, colleagues and others. Therefore they are aware that they must think and practise ethically at all times, and they acknowledge their right to stand by these principles and not be swayed from them.

Activity: Ethical principles

What is your initial response to the principles identified above? Can you identify times in helping practice where these may come into conflict with each other?

The examples listed below serve to illustrate how there may, at times, be a tension between ethical principles and counselling, coaching and mentoring practice with clients. In each case try to identify the principles which may be in conflict, and consider what you would do. Write down your responses, as we will come back to this activity later when we have considered a model to assist ethical decision making.

- You are employed as a coach in an organisation. An employee who you regularly see asks you to write them a reference for a new job. They don't want to ask their manager for a reference because they don't think that she will write anything positive: 'You'll say nice things about me, won't you?'

- You are a counsellor and your client discloses that she is the perpetrator of domestic violence. You have built up a relationship of trust with her, but you believe that her partner is at risk of harm.
- You are working as a mentor in a school. A pupil seeks you out to tell you that the young person you have been working with is a regular self-harmer and their friend is worried. Self-harm has not been discussed in mentoring sessions: you are still building a relationship of trust with your mentee.
- You are a drugs worker. One of the stipulations of working with clients is that they cannot relapse on more than three occasions. If they do, they will no longer be offered support. Your client discloses that she has used drugs for the fourth time, following the breakdown of her relationship. She begs you not to tell the organisation. She has been making good progress and you have a strong therapeutic relationship.
- Your client has come to the end of their six weeks' counselling with you in your voluntary agency. They have found it so helpful they ask if it would be OK to meet up for a chat every so often.
- You work for a telephone counselling agency. A client rings you at 3am saying they are going to throw themselves off a bridge in town and end their life.
- You work as a life-coach in private practice. One of your clients has applied for a job with an employer you know well. Your client asks you to 'put in a good word'. You do not feel that the client has the skills or experience to do the job for which they have applied.
- You are a social worker who has been asked to write a report on a client. You know that your client has disclosed something that could be potentially harmful for them if it came to light, but the disclosure was only made once, and then subsequently denied by the client. This client has made real progress during the time you have been working with them. Will you include the disclosure in the report?
- You are mentoring a client and feeling out of your depth at the issues being raised. You feel that it would help to talk about this to someone else in your organisation. But you have agreed with your client that the relationship is confidential.
- You start to see a client who discloses that she was abused by her previous counsellor. This has caused significant damage to her, but she does not want to make an official complaint to the professional body.

We will revisit these scenarios and your responses a little later. But first it is important to be aware that, alongside our knowledge and understanding of the ethical principles that underpin our practice, we are also guided by the ethical standards and codes of practice which apply to our professional contexts.

Ethical codes of practice

Ethical codes govern professional helping practice (counselling, coaching and mentoring) and it is to these that helpers should refer when they are working in helping relationships with clients. In addition, employers will also produce their own guidelines and regulations for ethical working, and helpers must ensure that they are familiar with the detail of these before engaging in helping practice. The organisations listed below are the main professional bodies which have a responsibility for overseeing ethical practice in the helping professions in the UK.

- Association for Coaching (AC)
- Association for Professional Executive Coaching and Supervision (APECS)
- British Association for Counselling and Psychotherapy (BACP)
- Counselling Psychology Division of the British Psychological Society (BPS)
- European Mentoring and Coaching Council (EMCC)
- International Coach Federation (ICF)
- United Kingdom Council for Psychotherapy (UKCP)

Although there are differences in the detail of the codes of practice developed by these professional bodies, key themes are evident. Cox, Bachkirova and Clutterbuck (2014), writing about coaching and mentoring codes of practice, identify five shared principles:

- Do not cause harm to others.
- Care for and act to promote the welfare of others.
- Practise within your own capabilities; know the limits of your competence.
- Pay attention to and value the interests of the client.
- Pay attention to and respect the law.

Bond (2015), writing from a counselling perspective, identifies seven shared features in the codes of practice of professional counselling bodies:

- The safety of the client.
- The professional competence of the counsellor.
- The need to respect differences in lifestyles, beliefs and values between clients.
- The prohibition of exploiting clients.
- The importance of contracting.

- The need for confidentiality.
- The responsibility to maintain the profession's reputation.

The link between the key themes identified above in coaching, mentoring and counselling contexts and the ethical principles outlined earlier in the chapter is clear. Non-maleficence and beneficence are embedded in each code of practice, whilst features that include working competently and working within boundaries of confidentiality and the law come into focus where they have not previously been referred to explicitly as an ethical principle. When helpers are engaging with people's lives, there is huge potential to abuse their positions of trust – not necessarily knowingly or deliberately or with malevolent intent, but simply because trying to do what is 'best' is not always straightforward. There are not enough words available here to enable a deep exploration of these elements. But it is important to note that contracting and confidentiality are paramount in ethical working. These concepts are explored in detail in Chapter 5.

A model for ethical decision making

To assist helpers in ensuring best ethical practice with clients, Bond (2015) proposes a model which offers a useful framework and 'step-by-step' guide to helpers. He identifies six stages which helpers can follow to assist them when they identify ethical dilemmas. These stages can be followed by asking the following questions:

1. *What is the dilemma?* Briefly describe the main elements of the dilemma. Bond suggests that sometimes just by speaking or writing a clear description of the problem or dilemma, it will no longer present as a dilemma and the action required will become clear.
2. *Whose dilemma is it?* Bond makes the point that helpers are responsible for the process and methods of helping, whereas clients are responsible for outcomes. It is not therefore the helper's duty to take responsibility for their clients' actions. Once helpers remind themselves of this, they may find that the dilemma ceases to become a dilemma. That said, Bond cautions us that in some cases – working with children and young people, for example – helpers may have responsibility for their clients when they are at risk of significant harm. Where this is the case, the dilemma becomes the counsellors' and needs further exploration.
3. *What do my ethical code of practice and my organisation's guidelines say?* This stage focuses on becoming as well informed as possible about the particular dilemma the counsellor, coach or mentor is facing. Helpers will want to ensure that they are practising within

the law, that they are not contravening any organisational policies, and that they are adhering to the ethical principles and ethical codes of practice. At this stage helpers may want to seek guidance from their organisation or their professional body, but being mindful at the same time of ensuring confidentiality to the client.

4. *What possible courses of action might I take?* It can be useful, at this stage, to identify as many courses of action as possible that are open to the helper. By so doing, counsellors, coaches and mentors can ensure that they are considering every way possible to resolve the dilemma.

5. *What is the best course of action to take?* Once helpers have thought through all the options available to them, they can evaluate which course of action will be most appropriate in this case. Stadler (1986) suggests three tests for selecting the best course of action:

   o *Universality* – would I recommend this course of action to others? Would I agree with the course of action if it had been taken by someone else?
   o *Publicity* – could I explain and justify my action to others? Would I be happy for my actions to be scrutinised publicly by others?
   o *Justice* – would I take the same action for other clients in similar situations? Would I take the same action if the client were influential or a celebrity, for example?

6. *What was the outcome of the action?* Once action has been taken, helpers should take time to reflect on and evaluate the outcome and ask themselves what has been achieved and whether they would take the same action again in similar circumstances.

It is important to note, once again, that the process of supervision for professional practice is crucial to enable deep reflection. When ethical dilemmas occur, the stages outlined above can be 'worked through' with a supervisor to ensure that the action taken is both ethical and lawful. Chapter 9 explores the concept and practice of supervision in detail.

Activity: Ethical dilemmas revisited

In the light of what you have read, return to the ten ethical dilemmas that you worked through earlier. Revisit each dilemma using Bond's six-stage model to work through a process of ethical decision making. Pay particular attention to Stadler's three tests for taking action: Would you recommend this course of action to others? Would you be happy for your actions to be scrutinised and made public to others? Would you take the same action for a person of influence or someone well-known?

Ethical practice with clients – personal reflection

As suggested throughout this chapter, the concept of ethics is a philosophical one. You will have surmised by now that there are no single correct answers when faced with ethical dilemmas; the helper must draw on their own morals and values, whilst adhering to their professional code of practice. Even then, decision making around appropriate action to take can be complex and is rarely straightforward. What follows includes a further selection of scenarios to enable you to reflect on your own moral and ethical thinking and to consider how you would respond when faced with dilemmas in your helping practice.

Activity: Reflection on ethical practice

Using what you have learned in this chapter, consider the scenarios outlined below. Identify (perhaps by scoring 1–10) which would be most problematic for you. These dilemmas do not all refer to client work; some are examples of dilemmas that helpers may face in relation to the demands of their organisation. What would you do if ...

- You are working as a mentor in a school. You are due to see a pupil with whom you have been working regularly. The relationship has been slow to build but trust has now been established. Your line manager tells you that you have to complete a report that is overdue and cancel your appointment with the pupil at the last minute.
- You are working as a counsellor in private practice. A friend is anxious about her teenage daughter. The friend asks you if you will take her daughter on as a client.
- A young client in school runs out of the counselling room in distress and leaves the building.
- You are a coach in private practice. Your client has left sessions on three occasions without paying. Each time, she apologises profusely and says she will 'bring the money next time'.
- You are working as a mentor in an organisation. The colleague you are mentoring discloses that she regularly takes days off work 'sick' in order to complete assignments that she is writing for her part-time degree course.
- You are a telephone helpline counsellor. A client rings in and tells you that he has sexually abused his daughter.
- A client you have been counselling for some while tells you that they are attracted to you. You have become aware that you are also feeling attracted to them.

(Continued)

(Continued)

- An elderly, terminally ill client you are supporting discloses that he has asked his wife to support him in ending his own life by suffocating him. His wife has agreed.
- A client arrives for counselling under the influence of alcohol. Your organisation has a policy of not counselling clients who have been drinking. Your client begs you not to turn them away: they have experienced a very traumatic situation which is why they felt they needed a drink.
- You are a school counsellor. The school has a strict policy on not giving lifts to pupils. You see one of your clients standing in the dark on a wet night, waiting for a bus. You know that you pass by his house and could drop him off at home on your way.

These scenarios offer the opportunity to reflect on which of the situations outlined would be most challenging. Although it is uncommon that these situations will arise, it is helpful to consider what you might do if they did. Once more, it is important to be aware of the place of supervision in supporting you to work ethically in helping practice.

Summary

This chapter set out to define and explore the concept of ethics and to establish the part that ethical thinking and decision making play in helping practice. The point has been made throughout that ethics is a complex and challenging element in professional helping relationships. It is important to end, once again, by stressing the need to make use of the full range of support mechanisms that are in place to assist you when ethical dilemmas occur. Knowledge of our own ethical principles – coupled with our professional body's code of practice and our organisation's policy and procedures on ethical working – will help to inform and support our ethical decision making. Our ability to reflect deeply and to use supervision effectively will ensure that we are able to adhere to Stadler's three tests of universality, publicity and justice when faced with ethical dilemmas.

Further reading suggestions

Banks, S. (2012) *Ethics and Values in Social Work* (4th edn). Basingstoke: Palgrave – Although this book focuses on social work practice, it nevertheless offers a useful introduction and insight into defining ethics and values.

Bond, T. (2015) *Standards and Ethics for Counselling in Action* (4th edn). London: Sage – An absolute must for professional helpers and particularly those training or practising as counsellors.

Cox, E., Bachkirova, T. and Clutterbuck, D. (2014) *The Complete Handbook of Coaching* (2nd edn). London: Sage – Chapter 30 offers a comprehensive and accessible overview of ethical practice in coaching.

8

WORKING WITH DIVERSITY

Chapter objectives: Readers will have the opportunity to ...

- define key terms and concepts underpinning diversity.
- identify how gender, class, culture, race, ethnicity, dis/ability and other factors are central to the life experience and development of every human being.
- consider their own responses to diversity in the helping context.
- reflect on effective ways of working with diversity in counselling, coaching and mentoring relationships.

Introduction

The ways in which our world and our worldview have changed over the last century are remarkable. The advent of accessible and relatively fast transport systems worldwide has meant that there is much greater mobility for individuals across cities, counties, countries and continents. In addition, the developments in technologies – particularly access to news about activities taking place through social media – have led to a significant increase in the availability of information and comment concerning issues and events as they unfold across the world. These factors have resulted in a heightened awareness of difference: difference between social and cultural backgrounds; difference between ethnic groups; difference between religious belief systems; difference in sexuality; difference between genders; difference in physical and cognitive abilities; difference between class; and so on. For those whose work is to engage with individuals in a helping relationship – counselling, coaching and mentoring – it is necessary to develop an increased awareness of what 'difference' is and what it means in the context of the work. To meet the individual needs of each and every client with whom they engage, helpers should ensure that issues of difference or 'diversity' are at the forefront of reflection on their practice.

This chapter sets out to define the key terms – diversity, discrimination, multiculturalism, equality, inclusion and integration – and to examine what these concepts mean in the context of helping practice. It will focus on individual differences and explore how every person's life is formed and informed by external factors as well as by their own innate genetic characteristics. The chapter will make suggestions for effective and sensitive ways of working with diversity. As with other chapters in this book, you will be invited to reflect on your own responses to issues of diversity. As with ethics (see previous chapter), the subject of diversity can raise powerful feelings, often to do with prejudice and stereotyping. Most helpers would agree that they adhere to the core conditions of a person-centred approach in their work (empathy, congruence and unconditional positive regard), but to demonstrate empathy with a client whose background is totally alien to that of the helper can be challenging. Showing unconditional positive regard to, say, a client whose radical religious beliefs may be abhorrent to the helper – whilst remaining congruent (genuine and 'real') during interactions with the client – is likely to require great reflection, reflexivity and skilled intervention on the part of the helper.

The case studies in Part II of this book provide examples of helpers working with clients across different contexts and from a range of backgrounds, where issues of diversity and equality are a central feature of the work. Each case study demonstrates the helper's sensitivity and awareness to issues of diversity. Take time to read these short case studies now, or when you reach the end of this chapter, with the word 'diversity' at the forefront of your thinking as you digest each real-life scenario. What issues of 'difference' might be raised for you if you were working with these clients?

Defining the terms

There is a plethora of terms associated with the overarching concept of diversity. The meanings attached to these terms can sometimes be 'woolly', confusing, easily misunderstood or even contested. For example, the concept of 'equality' does not, as we might surmise on first reading of the word, mean treating every individual equally. Rather it refers to ensuring a level playing field for everyone, which is different to treating every person in exactly the same way. This may mean responding differently to individuals with particular needs in order to ensure that the playing field can be levelled so that access to opportunity is fair. A simple example of equality would be the installation of ramps, to ensure equal access to public buildings for wheelchair users or for those with disabilities that affect mobility and who are unable to negotiate stairs to access the premises. An added complication to an already complex subject is that meanings relating to equality are often misinterpreted, and a 'right way' to approach issues of diversity is not universally acknowledged. More on this later. First, let us explore the terminology more fully.

Activity: Defining the terms

Reflect on the list of terms associated with equality of opportunity below. Beside each, note down your own brief definition and reflect on what the differences between the terms are. For example, how does integration differ from multiculturalism?

- Equality
- Diversity
- Inclusion
- Multiculturalism
- Integration
- Discrimination

We will go on to define each of these terms in detail. To begin, Bond (2015: 200) suggests three key definitions for social diversity:

- *Equality* – where every person has equal rights and a fair chance. It is an approach where there is recognition that different people have different starting points.
- *Diversity* – diverse means varied or different. We are different from each other so diversity includes us all. The concept of diversity encompasses acceptance and respect. It means both recognising that each individual is unique and understanding differences within that person's background.
- *Inclusion* – where every person feels respected, valued and that they have a contribution to make.

Bond makes it clear that *equality* is about ensuring fairness if a situation is deemed unfair and rights are not equal. He emphasises here that all human beings are diverse in that each and every one of us is different:

our physical appearance, upbringing, class, culture, sexuality, beliefs, values, experiences, thoughts, feelings and so on combine to produce a unique individual. So the concept of *diversity* applies to us all. He also reminds us of the need to demonstrate respect to each member of society, however different their situation and circumstances may be from our own, to ensure that they feel *included* and valued.

Multiculturalism and *integration* are both terms that refer to ways of ensuring that diversity is acknowledged and that inclusion in society is enhanced. Multiculturalism seeks to recognise, understand and embrace the diversity within any given society. Many countries across the world, the UK being one example, have taken a multicultural approach to diversity. But the concept and practice of multiculturalism, it could be argued, has become increasingly problematic; the recent rise in radicalism of different cultural and religious groups has prompted heightened levels of anxiety regarding terrorist activity across the world. This heightened anxiety is likely to result in greater suspicion and less acceptance of those who are 'different'. Simply put, multiculturalism attends to recognising, acknowledging and celebrating difference. Reid and Westergaard explain that:

> A multicultural approach seeks to develop an awareness of the potential impact of *any* social difference (for example, age, gender, social class, sexuality, ability or disability and so on). (2011: 61, emphasis in original)

They go on to caution against 'labelling' minority or marginalised groups in society, whilst acknowledging that 'refusing to discuss the needs of particular groups for fear of labelling them can undermine the collective experience of people who are marginalised and serves to conceal unequal power relationships' (2011: 61). An example of multiculturalism in practice in society might be the celebration of different faiths and cultures of pupils within a school setting, recognising the richness of the diversity within the school whilst giving pupils the opportunity to learn about and respect a range of cultural backgrounds that are different to their own.

Integration is also a response to diversity but, in contrast to multiculturalism, it seeks to ensure that individuals who may be marginalised or 'different' are assimilated into the 'receiving' society. In broad terms, a country that adopts a policy of integration will focus on enabling 'outsiders' to become 'insiders' by introducing them to the cultural norms within the dominant population and expecting that these norms are adopted. An example of this might be to focus less on recognising and celebrating the different faiths and cultures of pupils in a school, and more on putting strategies in place to ensure the pupils' swift integration – learning the dominant culture's language and faith, for example. These definitions are simplistic, but serve to illustrate the different approaches to diversity.

In helping practice, where professionals are engaging in one-to-one relationships with clients, it is important to be mindful of the need to recognise the 'whole person'. This involves working hard in the helping intervention to reflect on and understand all the factors and influences that make me 'me' and you 'you'. It is not about trying to make 'you' 'me'.

Various multicultural approaches to counselling have been developed (Sue *et al.*, 1996; Monk *et al.*, 2008; Arulmani, 2009) and one of these will be explored in more detail later in this chapter.

The final term in our list of concepts central to understanding the meaning of diversity, is *discrimination*. Although it is perhaps too simplistic to say that discrimination has the opposite meaning to equality, there is nevertheless some truth in that statement. Whereas equality seeks to ensure equal access to opportunities, discrimination (if done deliberately) sets out to ensure that some in society, for whatever reason – gender, ethnicity, class, disability and others – are excluded from certain opportunities. For example, it would be unlawful for a hotel to exclude gay, lesbian or bisexual couples on the grounds of their guests' sexuality. However, it would be within the law to set up a support group for women who are victims of domestic violence, which excludes men. In this example a large group in society is discriminated against on the grounds of gender, but this is lawful; the group members' vulnerability and experience of violent and abusive men has led society, through the law, to acknowledge the need for special consideration. Whereas in this example the discrimination is overt but within the law, it can also be indirect, unlawful and sometimes heavily 'disguised'. For instance, many people who apply for employment when over the age of 55 suspect that their applications are not treated fairly; the employer may notice their age and be reluctant to take on someone who is likely to work in the organisation for a limited amount of time. Although some mature applicants appear to meet all the criteria and specifications of the job, they are still not invited for interview.

The Equality Act 2010, applicable to the UK, protects against discrimination and recognises this practice as unlawful. It lists a comprehensive range of identifying characteristics against which individuals may not be discriminated. These are:

- Age
- Disability
- Gender reassignment
- Marriage/civil partnership
- Race
- Religion or belief
- Sex
- Sexual orientation

It is important for helpers to familiarise themselves with the law in order to be able to support clients who may be the victims of discrimination and to ensure that they are not colluding with, or even practising, discrimination themselves in the helping relationship. Helpers who advertise their services, particularly those in private practice, should be aware of their own anti-discriminatory responsibilities when accepting clients for counselling, coaching or mentoring. The United Kingdom Council for Psychotherapy (2009) looks further than the legal characteristics of what can constitute discrimination listed above, and adds protected categories which include colour, social, economic or immigration status, and lifestyle.

Activity: Reviewing the terms

Revisit the previous activity in the light of what you have just read. Are there definitions that you would like to change? Amend?

In addition to the terminology identified and defined above, there are other, less helpful terms that are associated with diversity. One that will be familiar is the notion of 'political correctness', often used to denigrate those who are striving for greater inclusivity, respect and understanding, and are mindful of the impact of their words and actions on others. Another word that at first glance might appear to be acceptable and inclusive is 'tolerance'. However, to be 'tolerant' implies a power dynamic where one society or individual tolerates but does not necessarily engage directly with, wholly accept or embrace another. Tolerance is not the same as acceptance, and the two terms should not be confused. Helpers, by the very definition of the word, should strive to be mindful, respectful and accepting towards every client with whom they engage, rather than simply being tolerant of who they are.

Diversity and its impact

It is helpful to be clear about the terms and concepts associated with the subject of diversity. It is important too to develop an accurate understanding of how the factors that both unite us and set us apart also help to form each unique individual and inform how we respond to each other. Knowledge of factors forming our own identity, and of how our 'differences' are perceived and responded to by others, is central to helping practice. Barriers to engagement between ourselves and our clients might exist, of which we as helpers may be unaware. Once we can become aware of and understand these factors more fully, we will be better placed to engage at some relational depth with each client and to understand why our clients may, at times, find it hard to engage with us.

Activity: What makes me 'me'?

Take a moment to list all the characteristics that identify you as 'you'. The list below might act as a starting point. What are your defining features?

- Name
- Gender
- Ethnicity
- Colour
- Class
- Religious beliefs
- Dis/ability
- Sexuality
- Cultural influences
- Family systems

Using the characteristics identified above as a guide, write a statement about yourself that starts with the words 'I would describe myself as ...'

This activity demonstrates the complexity of the elements that contribute to our identity. The simple issue of our name and where it came from can be hugely significant in helping us to answer the question 'Who do I think I am?' Thompson (2011) identifies the part that our personal, cultural and social characteristics play in forming us and in influencing our responses to others. He also makes the challenging but accurate point that by simply 'being' *who* we are, we may be perceived as oppressive to another, even though we are not setting out to oppress and we consider ourselves to be accepting of difference. For example, in the 20th century some separatist feminist groups argued that all men were oppressive to women – just by being men. It could be suggested that society has 'moved on' and there is greater acceptance of difference; however, there are still significant characteristics that may be perceived as oppressive by one person – but not another. In helping practice, awareness of, and striving for, anti-oppressive practice is paramount. The example below serves to illustrate this point. George, the counsellor, describes his feelings about working with Jamelia. She also talks about how it feels to have George as her counsellor.

Case study: George (counsellor) and Jamelia – oppression in the helping relationship

George: 'I've been working with Jamelia for a number of sessions. She seems reluctant to engage with me at times: she is very quiet and often looks away when I speak to her. Our relationship has developed, but I believe that Jamelia is not being totally open with me. She is unable to trust me yet. I'm sure that this will build in time. She is an interesting client with a fascinating story to tell.'

Jamelia: 'I've been seeing George for counselling. I'm sure that he is a lovely man. He is kind and I like him. But I don't believe that he will ever understand what has happened to me – my life as a refugee, running from an oppressive regime – and it makes it hard for me to open up and talk to him. He is older than me, a white man, educated and probably not used to meeting people like me. Apart from anything else, I'm not used to talking to men who are not family members. He wears a suit. He reminds me of the people I met when I first arrived here. Official and a bit scary.'

As stated above, oppressive practice is not always deliberate. George does not set out to oppress Jamelia. He acknowledges that Jamelia does not trust him in the relationship but is confident that, in time, she will do so. He does not appear to recognise or identify specifically the differences between them that may be oppressive to Jamelia and may present a barrier to their engagement. Trust between Jamelia and George may build if George is able to reflect deeply, but then again it may not. This is not because George is deliberately taking an oppressive stance, but simply that the characteristics that he possesses, over which he has no control and is unable to change – white, male, middle-aged – represent issues of power for Jamelia that make it very hard for her to build trust and open up to her counsellor. Later we will consider how we can work in ways that will help to ameliorate anti-oppressive practice. But first let us explore this concept further with some practical examples.

Activity: Oppression in helping relationships

Consider the list below and identify what potential issues of diversity or even oppression might be perceived in each case. What might the client be feeling? What might the helper be feeling? What might you be feeling with each client presented below?

(Continued)

(Continued)

- A white middle-aged heterosexual female counsellor working with a young black man who is homosexual.
- An able-bodied male life-coach working with a young man who has recently been discharged from the armed forces because of an accident that has left him wheelchair bound.
- A black male mentor in a school setting working with a young Muslim woman who wears a niqab.
- A black female evangelical Christian mentor working with a black working-class young male offender with no faith.
- A young, newly qualified female counsellor working with a couple in their 60s who are experiencing sexual difficulties in their relationship.
- A coach working with a colleague in an organisation, where the coach is also the colleague's line manager.
- A young white working-class male counsellor working in an independent private girls' school.
- A black middle-aged middle-class drugs counsellor working with a white working-class heroin addict.
- A Sikh male counsellor working with a young black woman who is questioning her sexuality.
- A newly qualified mentor from Eastern Europe with a strong accent, working in a school in a rural area for young people with social, emotional and behavioural difficulties.

The scenarios outlined above demonstrate that diversity and perceived oppression may have an impact on the helping relationship. Of course, it might be that in the case of every scenario detailed, helper and client are able to form a therapeutic relationship and that issues of oppression do not feature. But it is important to acknowledge that the perceptions clients have about helpers, and likewise that helpers have about their clients, will come into play in the dynamic of every relationship and it is therefore important to acknowledge and be transparent about difference. Reid and Westergaard explain:

> As there is no concept of what is 'normal' a starting point in any counselling relationship is to take account of 'difference' on *both* sides of the relationship and be willing to talk about cultural issues at the start of the process. What is important here is to take account of the client's views and work to their preferences rather than making stereotypical decisions about what will work best for certain groups. (2011: 63, emphasis in original)

In the testimony below, Sue, an experienced career counsellor, demonstrates her lack of understanding about diversity and the

potential for oppressive practice as she talks about her work in a girls'
school located in a geographical area with a high population of Asian
students.

> ## Case study: Sue (career counsellor)
>
> I'm finding it very difficult to engage with the pupils in this school. I've
> never experienced this before in other schools where I've worked. The
> girls here often don't look at me in their career sessions, which is strange,
> and it makes me think that they're just not engaging. Most seem very
> ambitious and want to enter careers in medicine or law without knowing
> anything about those areas of work. Some just don't seem interested in
> talking about their future at all. One 18-year-old pupil told me that there
> was no point in having a career interview because she would be moving
> back to Bangladesh to marry someone she has never met! Honestly! What
> a way to live.

Sue is sharing her experiences without any apparent awareness of
diversity. She appears not to be able to engage with her clients as individual and unique human beings, and demonstrates little understanding
of their cultural backgrounds, but rather takes a stereotypical and
unhelpful viewpoint. If she took more time to explore the cultural and
social factors which underpin many of her clients' lives, she might
understand better the reasons why some of the young women do not
engage with eye contact. She may also learn about the possible underlying cultural reasons why many of the young women she sees appear
to have decided on careers in medicine and law. Reid summarises these
points clearly:

> Of course, what we see in others depends very much on where we
> stand to look. Our particular stance needs to be understood in terms
> of its social and historical origins. (2015: 136)

So, if issues of diversity are central to engagement and the work of the
professional helper, how do we ensure that we acknowledge and work
effectively and empathetically with 'difference' with our clients?

Working with diversity – a helping model

As established earlier in the chapter, there are a number of models
which can be applied to working with diversity, particularly in relation

to culture, in the helping context. The model we will explore here is that developed by Sue *et al.* (1996). Although introduced some time ago, the model still holds credence and is relevant and helpful to professional practice in counselling, coaching and mentoring. What follows is a brief description of their cross-cultural skills matrix, developed for the counselling context but equally applicable in coaching and mentoring relationships. The matrix is organised using three headings:

1. Our awareness of the assumptions, beliefs and values that we hold.
2. Our ability to engage with and understand the worlds of 'culturally different' clients.
3. Our willingness to learn about and develop appropriate strategies and techniques.

Reid (2015), drawing on the work of D'Andrea and Daniels (1991), suggests four levels of competency in helping relationships which relate to the above headings. She identifies these as:

1. *Culturally entrenched* – counsellors who believe that all that is needed to engage is the ability to listen and to demonstrate unconditional positive regard, empathy and genuineness to every client in a helping relationship. As every client is a unique individual, cultural differences are 'risen above'.
2. *Cross-cultural awakening* – counsellors acknowledge that there may be cultural differences, but focus on the similarities in order to reduce 'difference' and to establish consistency across client groups. This means seeing a client's point of view whilst acknowledging it as 'different' to our own.
3. *Cultural integrity* – acknowledging that a range of skills may be applied in order to meet the needs of different cultural groups. This may mean developing a new vocabulary or thinking in a different way.
4. *Infusion* – a multicultural approach becomes embedded. This is not simply the case of a counsellor adapting skills and techniques for a particular client group, but involves challenging our own worldview and opening ourselves up to the values and beliefs of others.

We will take a moment to pause here and reflect on our own competence in multicultural practice. It is important to be aware of our own level of competence in relation to diversity and to consider what we need to do in order to develop our multicultural competence further.

Activity: Multicultural competence – where am I?

Consider your own multicultural competence in helping relationships using the levels outlined above. If you are already in practice, try to identify a time when you came into contact with a client from a cultural background with which you were unfamiliar. Using the four levels of competence outlined here, where would you place your response to the client? If you are not yet working with clients, try to imagine this situation. How might you respond?

Reid and Westergaard suggest some development points to ensure greater cultural understanding. These are presented in the form of 'principles' for multicultural practice and are informed by Sue *et al.*'s matrix. These principles serve to encourage helpers to consider how they might develop their levels of multicultural competency. In the list below, Reid and Westergaard (2011: 72–3) are writing specifically for the counselling context with young people. However, the principles listed here apply equally in other helping contexts and are relevant to adult client work. These principles include:

- awareness of own biases and limitations and their outcomes;
- recognition of the range of social variables that lead to cultural difference;
- knowledge about the causes and effects of oppression, racism, discrimination and stereotyping;
- openness about the processes of counselling young people with a view to a collaborative approach that works alongside the young person;
- commitment to enriching understanding through continuous personal and reflexive development;
- searching for appropriate and culturally sensitive models of intervention, rather than reliance on established or 'singular' methods;
- awareness and understanding of the impact of negative treatment experienced by marginalised groups;
- commitment to outreach work;
- respect for young people's beliefs, values and views about themselves and the stories they choose to tell the counsellor;
- valuing the language, style and manner of speech, whilst acknowledging that there will be times when the counsellor's linguistic skills will be inadequate;
- questioning of the appropriateness and helpfulness of organisational assessment methods;

- awareness of institutional practices that lead to discrimination;
- congruence when advocating with or lobbying on behalf of young people to overcome relevant discrimination;
- understanding of the differences in communication styles and their impact, plus extension of own communication skills and methods;
- open-mindedness to alternative ways of supporting, including using the resources of the young person's community.

Activity

Take a moment to reflect on the principles listed above. What is your response to this list of principles? To what extent are you committed to them? Which of these, if any, would pose a particular challenge for you? What action might you take to go about developing these principles further in your practice? And now return to the previous case study of Sue. Which of the principles outlined above do you think she needs to attend to and work on in her career counselling practice?

The list of principles detailed above may at first glance appear daunting to the newly qualified and practising helper. The intention is not to suggest that helpers work so hard focusing on and embedding cultural awareness that they lose sight of what it is they are working to achieve from a therapeutic perspective. What is central here is an openness to acknowledging diversity and talking about it with clients to enable greater understanding. A simple question – 'I'm wondering how it feels to be sitting in this room with me?' – can serve to open up a conversation about difference and ensure that greater understanding is established. The listening skills which are central to all helping practice, will be used by the helper to heighten their awareness of verbal and non-verbal messages communicated by their client. These clues are important in helping us to build a greater understanding about our client's world and their worldview.

Talbot, Pahlevan and Boyles illustrate how the principles above are applied in their practice. They describe their work as counsellors and counselling interpreters with torture survivors seeking asylum in the UK. As helpers, they do not share a common language with their clients, yet they must build an accurate understanding of their clients' experiences and their emotional and psychological states, whilst enabling them to move on. They discuss the challenges of having an interpreter in the counselling room, whilst acknowledging that without the interpreter present, counselling would not be available to these clients with extreme needs. They make the point that:

> As trust builds, the client's attention is naturally drawn to the thera-pist and away from the interpreter, and the interpreter's presence diminishes or fades. They are still fully present, but discreetly so, reflecting the tone and manner of the therapist and transferring the feeling and meaning behind the narrative of the client. (Talbot et al., 2015: 14)

Whilst recognising the need for cultural awareness and sensitivity, it is also important to be clear that in Europe and North America the empha-sis is frequently on an integrative approach to helping, where person-centred principles which value clients' autonomy and responsibil-ity for decision making prevail. Here, a note of caution must be sounded. Bond (2015) reminds us that our 'Western' understanding of counselling may require significant modification in order to address the needs of other cultures. He explains that counselling which requires reflexivity and searches for meaning 'may struggle to meet the needs of many people from traditional cultures in Africa and Asia ... where authoritative or expert advice may be more greatly valued than being supported to think reflexively by the counsellor' (2015: 204). Helen George illustrates this point clearly when writing about her research into barriers to counselling for older African Caribbean women in the UK, suffering with mental health issues. She explains that 'resistance to opening up and talking about problems is a powerful cultural norm that's entrenched in African Caribbean women' (2015: 14). She goes on to conclude that:

> With those women who still do not feel able to seek help, we need, perhaps, to respect their privacy and cultural norms of 'not talking their business' and consider other ways that they can be supported so that they don't have to continue to suffer in silence. (2015: 16)

Cox, Bachkirova and Clutterbuck highlight the paradox inherent in what they describe as 'cross-cultural' coaching. They illustrate this paradox by suggesting that at times it is possible to 'deal explicitly and primarily with culture as a variable and an influence in coaching', but that at the same time, 'doing cross-cultural coaching is theoretically dubious and can be highly perilous' (2014: 345). The point here is that whilst sensitivity to and awareness of cultural factors is important, a relentless focus on culture may mask other variables and issues that need attention.

To conclude, I have set out a list of simple, straightforward and help-ful guidelines which will encourage you to reflect further upon and respond appropriately to issues of diversity in your helping practice. These suggestions serve to offer a practical starting point for helpers when working with 'difference' in their practice.

- Acknowledge difference.
- Be aware of your own prejudices and stereotypical judgements.
- Be mindful of the importance of developing anti-oppressive practice in the helping relationship; how might your client perceive you?
- Be open about difference: How does it feel to the client? How does it feel to you?
- Research the cultural norms of a particular marginalised group when people from this group are likely to include your clients.
- Use supervision to reflect on and discuss issues of diversity.
- Finely hone and utilise active-listening skills to develop a full understanding of your clients' responses – verbal and non-verbal.

By using the above points as a practical guide, you will be mindful of the need to work with diversity sensitively and transparently. We often fear what we do not know, and working with difference can, initially, appear daunting. Once we accept the richness and complexity of the human race – the personal, social and cultural factors that define us – then we can truly engage fully and confidently in helping relationships with a range of clients.

Summary

Working with diversity is a challenging subject. Helpers must become aware of the significance of the uniqueness of every individual – and the factors that contribute to this uniqueness – as they engage with clients. The chapter set out to define the terms associated with diversity and to explore their meaning in relation to the helping professions. You have had the opportunity to reflect on your own identity when considering what factors (personal, cultural and social) make you the person you are. Furthermore, the concept of anti-oppressive practice was introduced and the ways in which oppression can be perceived in the helping relationship have been highlighted. Finally, a set of principles and guidelines for working with diversity has been suggested. As explained, what is presented here is a starting point for exploring this fascinating subject. The reading suggested below will offer a greater depth of analysis and will support you in further developing your knowledge in this field.

Further reading suggestions

Pedersen, P., Draguns, J.G., Lonner, W.J. and Trimble, J.E. (2008) *Counselling Across Cultures* (6th edn). Thousand Oaks, CA: Sage – This book is in its sixth edition and continues to provide a valuable resource to counsellors.

Rosinski, P. (2003) *Coaching Across Cultures: New Tools for Leveraging National, Corporate and Professional Differences*. London: Nicholas Brealey – A text on diversity from a coaching perspective, with many examples.

Thompson, N. (2011) *Promoting Equality: Working with Diversity and Difference* (3rd edn). Basingstoke: Palgrave Macmillan – A really useful and practical guide which explores a range of issues regarding equality and diversity.

9

SUPERVISION AND CONTINUING PROFESSIONAL DEVELOPMENT FOR HELPERS

Chapter objectives: Readers will have the opportunity to ...

- define the terms 'supervision' and 'continuing professional development' in the helping professions;
- identify the key functions of supervision – formative, normative and restorative;
- consider how to engage effectively with and get the most from supervision and a range of continuing professional development opportunities.

Introduction

Anyone who works to develop professional helping relationships – whether as counsellor, coach or mentor – is likely to face issues that sadden, confuse, frustrate, surprise, anger, excite or even frighten them at times. Engaging with the detail and complexity of another person's life will often resonate with, and bring to the forefront, issues we are facing in our own lives. Sometimes it can be difficult to differentiate between what is our emotional 'stuff' and what belongs to our clients. In this climate of heightened emotions (the exploration of clients' challenging and complex issues and our own personal responses to their stories) it is important that helpers are given the support they need to 'unpack', reflect on and 'process' the work. This in-depth reflection and exploration will ensure that helpers can continue to be of assistance to their clients, whilst recognising and managing their own feelings effectively. Supervision – a key activity in counselling, coaching and mentoring – provides professional helpers with a safe environment to reflect on and develop best practice, and at the same time offers them a time and place both to share their concerns, fears and frustrations, and to consider strategies for continuing to work effectively with their clients.

This chapter encourages readers to appreciate the purpose and functions of supervision and other continuing professional development opportunities and activities (including research), and to consider how they can engage with these effectively. The chapter begins by defining the terms 'supervision' and 'continuing professional development'. It goes on to explore what supervision and continuing professional development opportunities are and how they can be used by helpers to enhance their professional practice. Readers will have the opportunity to reflect on their own personal and professional development and to consider how professional development opportunities might be used effectively. This chapter draws heavily on Reid and Westergaard's (2013) *Effective Supervision for Counsellors*, where supervision is explored in detail.

Supervision and continuing professional development – defining the terms

The term 'supervision' can be problematic in professional helping practice, implying as it does a relationship where one person oversees and directs the work of another. The various dictionary definitions of the word each imply an 'expert overview' whereby a relationship of power is implicit: the supervisor instructs the supervisee and has responsibility for the supervisee's work. To illustrate this definition we can think about a supervisor overseeing the work of a checkout operator in a supermarket. Supervisors in this kind of work context are often called on to sort out problems, deal with customers, and override mistakes, and they can open the till manually – something that the till operator does not have the power to do. In many working contexts supervision denotes this kind of power relationship, where the supervisor has responsibility for their supervisee. It is important that we are clear that this is *not* the function of supervision in the helping professions. Here, the supervisor has responsibility *to*, not responsibility *for*, the professional helper. Let us explore this further.

Activity: What is supervision?

You may already be receiving supervision so this activity will be straightforward for you to undertake. It may be a little harder if you have yet to engage actively in a professional helping relationship and have not yet experienced supervision. I want you to note down your thoughts on what supervision is, what it sets out to achieve, and why it is considered necessary – even compulsory – in professional helping practice.

Although not every professional helping context demands that helpers receive mandatory supervision, many do, including counselling, some health professions, and social work. Even where supervision is not mandatory, it is becoming increasingly accepted that providing those who work to support others with a 'reflective space' themselves serves to ensure that they are engaged in best practice with their clients. For it is the welfare of the client, first and foremost, that receives attention in supervision; so supervision in the helping professions focuses on client practice. Supervisees will 'bring' their clients with them to supervision – not literally, of course – in order to reflect on and explore their work in depth and consider new strategies and different ways of working to ensure that their clients are moving forward and the work remains purposeful.

Reid and Westergaard clarify what supervision means to them:

> There is a well-known expression – a problem shared is a problem halved – and in many ways, at a very basic level, this sums up the process of both counselling and supervision. As a practising counsellor, I look forward to supervision, not only because it offers me a reflective learning space, but also [because it] provides an environment in which I can be open and honest about my thoughts and feelings concerning my client work. I often find myself approaching supervision sessions with a sense of heaviness, particularly when I am exposed to, or am 'containing', challenging or painful client material. I will frequently leave my supervision sessions with a lighter tread, a feeling that I have 'let go' of the burden, or rather that my supervisor is sharing the load with me. Having undertaken research with counsellors, I know I am not alone in these perceptions. On reflection, this is unsurprising. How many times have clients left counselling saying 'I feel so much better now I've told you about this,' whilst I exit the counselling room bearing the weight of what my client has shared with me? (2013: 170)

What is evident here is that the process of supervision attends to more than simply the 'oversight' of the helper – a counsellor in this case – but to their support too. It is not solely the welfare of the client that forms the focus, but also the well-being of the helper, as suggested above. One of the key concepts in supervision is that of the 'parallel process'. This means that what happens in supervision mirrors, to a greater or lesser extent, what takes place in the helping relationship between the supervisee and their clients. Hawkins and Shohet, writing about supervision in the broader helping professions, clarify this further and describe the ways in which supervision can be of benefit. The quote below illustrates the parallel process and, although it describes the relationship between the supervisor and supervisee, it can be applied equally to any helping relationship with clients. They explain that supervision can

> give us a chance to stand back and reflect; a chance to avoid the easy way out of blaming others – clients, peers, the organization, 'society' or even oneself; and it can give us a chance to engage in the search for new options, to discover the learning that often emerges from the most difficult situations, and to get support. (2000: 3)

So if supervision attends to more than simply the *oversight* of the helper, what exactly is its purpose? What does it set out to achieve? The BACP (2010: 2) clarifies the broad aims of supervision:

- To assist the development of the reflective practitioner.
- To support the therapist.
- To maximise the effectiveness of the therapeutic relationship.
- To monitor/safeguard the interests of the client.
- To maintain ethical standards as set out in the *Ethical Framework*.

Inskipp and Proctor (1993), who have written widely about counselling supervision, acknowledge these aims and identify how they are addressed within three key functions of supervision:

- Formative
- Normative
- Restorative

Others have identified similar functions but from slightly different professional contexts. Kadushin (1992), writing from a social work perspective, lists the functions as:

- Educative
- Administrative (managerial)
- Supportive

Meanwhile, Hawkins and Shohet (2006), focusing on supervision in the wider helping professions, suggest the terms:

- Developmental
- Qualitative
- Resourcing

The similarities between the terms in these three lists are greater than the differences. I prefer to use Inskipp and Proctor's definitions as they suggest a collaborative, process approach – something that is done together and is on-going – which reflects the true nature of the supervisory relationship. Each function will be explored further here.

The formative function

The formative function attends to the 'forming' of the supervisee. This focuses on their personal and professional development from both a 'macro' and 'micro' perspective. The broader, macro perspective is concerned with professional development opportunities that might support the supervisee in their client work, for example undertaking training which examines a new therapeutic technique, or enrolling on a course which focuses on bereavement counselling for a helper who is working with clients who happen to be experiencing loss. The 'micro' element of the formative function is also concerned with change and the development of the supervisee, but in relation to their individual client practice, for example exploring and gaining greater understanding about the key issues that a particular client is bringing, or considering a specific technique or strategy to adopt with a client who is feeling overwhelmed in a particular area.

Khaled, a life-coach, describes how the formative function was addressed effectively in his recent supervision session.

Case study: Khaled (life-coach) – the formative function of supervision

I was really struggling with one of my clients recently. I have seen her for a number of sessions but we were starting to feel so stuck – going round in circles and getting nowhere. When I 'brought' my client to supervision and started to talk through the issues I was facing, in particular the 'stuckness', I began to see that I was starting to try to 'fix' my client and 'solve' all her problems by making lots of suggestions which were all met by, 'Yes, but ...'

or, 'No, but …'. We talked in supervision about 'handing responsibility back' to the client, making greater use of the skill of summary, and focusing on using open and hypothetical questions in order to do this; and maybe even using immediacy to express and explore what is happening in the room between us. This really helped me to think about how I could develop my practice further and work more effectively with this client.

Khaled demonstrates the formative function in a 'micro' way – describing how supervision gave him the opportunity to reflect on this piece of client work objectively with his supervisor, and think about how to enable his client to become an active participant in her coaching sessions by using different techniques and strategies.

Activity: The formative function of supervision

Reflecting on your understanding of the formative function so far, make a list of the ways in which attending to the formative function of supervision might assist the helper to feel more confident in their client practice.

I am sure that your list included points such as:

- having a greater understanding about clients' issues, needs and challenges;
- developing insight into how to work more effectively with clients;
- finding out about and trying new strategies and techniques to use with clients;
- making links between theory and practice; applying theoretical perspectives to helping practice;
- engaging in training programmes and professional development opportunities to enhance helping practice;
- identifying relevant reading to assist new insights and understanding.

Whereas the formative function in supervision attends to the 'formation', education and development of the supervisee, the normative function has a different emphasis.

The normative function

Supervisors should always be mindful to ensure that their supervisees are working within the 'norms' of their organisation and are practising ethically and legally, adhering to organisational policies and demonstrating lawful practice at all times. I explained earlier in the chapter that supervisors are not responsible *for* their supervisees, but are responsible *to* them. This means that supervisors have an obligation to ensure that their supervisees' client practice is always best practice. They have a responsibility to enable supervisees to understand fully what constitutes best practice and to ensure that supervisees know what action they must take if ethical or lawful practice has been contravened. Like each of the functions of supervision, the normative function is all about supporting the supervisee to develop and make changes in their practice when necessary. That said, the supervisor must be very clear about their professional responsibilities towards their supervisee's clients. If a supervisor is concerned about an aspect of their supervisee's practice, they must take action. Initially, this action will involve addressing the concerns in supervision, but it may mean – if the supervisee does not act to make changes to their practice – explaining that confidentiality will be broken by the supervisor in order that the issue is addressed. Connie, a school counsellor, explains how the normative function supported her in her counselling work with a particular client.

Case study: Connie (school counsellor) – the normative function of supervision

I was talking to my supervisor about my work with my client, Robbie. I was starting to feel increasingly anxious about the things that Robbie was disclosing to me in our counselling sessions. I know that I have a responsibility to break confidentiality with clients if they are at risk of significant harm, but I wasn't sure if what Robbie was telling me fitted that category. It's all very well to know that it is my responsibility to break confidentiality when clients are at risk, but it is quite another thing to make the judgement about whether or not what they are telling me actually constitutes a risk of significant harm. In Robbie's case, this was a really 'grey area'. Just talking to my supervisor about this, and taking time away from Robbie to reflect on the things he had told me, helped me to see more clearly that I was, in fact, able to maintain confidentiality in his case. My supervisor is such a calm and objective presence. He really gives me the confidence to know that I am making sound decisions in my client work.

Connie is very clear, in the testimony above, that supervision – and in this case, the normative function in particular – helped to keep her practice safe.

Activity: The normative function of supervision

Reflecting on your understanding of the normative function so far, make a list of the ways in which attending to this function in supervision might assist the helper to feel more confident in their client practice.

It is likely that your list included the following:

- Clarity regarding the law, policy and ethical working.
- Reflecting on and acting appropriately when 'grey areas' emerge.
- Keeping safe in professional practice.
- Sharing issues that feel 'out of our depth'.

Whereas the formative function attends to the education and developmental needs of the supervisee, and the normative function focuses on supporting best ethical, lawful and professional practice, the restorative function is concerned with another important element of the work – the emotional and psychological support of the supervisee.

The restorative function

Having read this book and reflected on the case studies in Part II, one thing will have become clear: professional helping practice is complex, challenging and emotionally demanding work. Counsellors, coaches and mentors at the end of a working day are likely to feel tired, drained and sometimes even helpless or desperately sad. This is only to be expected when we have engaged at such emotional and relational depth with our clients. Supervision, then, attends to the emotional and psychological needs of the helper, 'restoring' their equilibrium and sense of well-being. The Reid and Westergaard quote earlier in this chapter made reference to the well-known expression 'A problem shared is a problem halved'. The restorative function is all about enabling helpers to share their 'problems', reflections, thoughts and feelings regarding their work with clients. The role of the supervisor here is to 'contain' and manage the emotional content, in much the same way as helpers do for their clients – the parallel process again. Luther, a workplace mentor, explains how the restorative function of supervision supported him through a challenging emotional time with one of his clients.

Case study: Luther (workplace mentor) – the restorative function of supervision

It was tough. I'd been mentoring Steve for a while and he was doing really well. Then one day, at our meeting, he broke down and told me that his work was really suffering because his marriage was at breaking point and he didn't know where to turn. He sobbed throughout our session. He was absolutely distraught and couldn't see a future for himself that didn't involve his partner. He couldn't think about work at all. I found it really difficult to just stay with Steve's pain. It was so hard to be alongside someone who was feeling so desperate. I wanted to reassure him that everything would be OK. But I wasn't sure that I actually had the power to say this. At the same time, what Steve was saying opened up issues for me, as two years ago my partner and I had gone through a really tricky time. I 'took' Steve to supervision. I was really surprised that I too broke down in my supervision session. It was as though I had 'held onto' Steve's pain whilst waiting for my supervision session, when I could let it all out. I felt so much better after supervision: lighter and clearer about my role in relation to Steve's situation. I don't know what I would have done without my supervisor. I'm not sure that I would have had the emotional strength to go back and see Steve again.

Luther's testimony illustrates how powerful – and painful sometimes – helping practice can be. He reminds us of the parallel process again: where what happened in the mentoring meeting with Steve was 'played out' again in the supervision room. Reflecting on the emotions experienced by helpers in their practice with clients is an essential element of the helping process. Often what we feel as helpers can serve to shed light on what our clients are experiencing and help us to consider how to continue to make the helping process valuable.

Activity: The restorative function of supervision

Reflecting on your understanding of the restorative function so far, make a list of the ways in which attending to this function in supervision might assist the helper to feel more confident in their client practice.

The restorative element of supervision is highly valued by helpers. Your list is likely to include the points detailed below:

- Dealing with our own emotional responses serves to illuminate and help us to process our client work.
- Ensuring our own emotional and psychological well-being is necessary in order to respond effectively to the needs of our clients.
- Reflexivity (a heightened awareness of our own emotional responses) and reflectivity are enhanced by a greater understanding of our own feelings.

The functions of supervision should now be clear and the purpose of the supervisory relationship in the professional helping context has been established. The benefits of this relationship should be evident to the supervisee, the organisation for which the supervisee works, and the clients with whom they engage. Let us think now about these benefits in a little more detail.

Activity: The benefits of supervision

Take a moment to list the possible benefits of supervision to the following:

- Supervisee
- Organisation/employer
- Client

The benefits of supervision to the supervisee have been set out in the analysis of the functions above. Supervisees should be supported to *form* and develop their practice from both a macro and micro perspective. They should be enabled to work within the *norms* of their organisation and the law, whilst ensuring best ethical practice. Finally, the emotional and psychological well-being of the supervisee is *restored* through the supervisory process. Where supervisees are employed in organisations, their work is supported by the supervisory process and good practice is encouraged. Furthermore, where supervisees feel valued and cared for, there is likely to be less stress and burn-out, and the organisation benefits as a result. The client should also benefit as – unbeknown to them – their helper is encouraged to reflect on the work and consider strategies to enable them to move forward.

Methods of supervision

The practical process of supervision can take many forms. There is insufficient space here to go into detail about different models of supervision, but the list below sets out some of the ways in which supervision can be delivered:

- One to one with an external supervisor.
- One to one with a line-manager supervisor.
- Group supervision facilitated by an external supervisor.
- Peer supervision with no identified supervisor.

There are pros and cons to each method. In particular, there is an on-going debate about the issues inherent in supervision facilitated by a line manager. Here there is already a power dynamic established that cannot be ignored; it may be difficult – or impossible – for a supervisee to bring a 'challenging' piece of work to reflect on in supervision, particularly if the supervisee is anxious that they have not demonstrated best practice in a specific piece of client work. Where line managers are involved in disciplinary procedures and have input into decisions about performance-related pay, it might also be difficult to develop a completely open and trusting relationship. Kirsty, a coach working in an organisation setting, reflects on her experiences of a range of different supervision models.

Case study: Kirsty (coach) – experiences of supervision using different methods

My first supervisor was external, paid for by my organisation to come in for a couple of hours every month to supervise me. I loved those sessions! I felt very safe to talk about my practice, knowing that she wasn't judging me. She helped me to reflect and to think about different ways of working. She also suggested books I could read that would help with my work. Those sessions were invaluable. A couple of years ago my organisation did a large restructure and they changed from external supervision to a line-manager model. Initially this was tricky. I didn't get on with my line manager and I certainly didn't feel safe enough with her to share my practice in any depth. Also, she was not a qualified coach herself, so I didn't really respect her judgements about my work. I found her a bit intimidating and bossy, to be honest – not like my first supervisor at all. When she left, I had a new line manager and supervision with him was great. Although he was my line manager, I could be open and honest with him – even about my mistakes. I also belong to a peer supervision group where the four coaches working in the organisation meet together. This is great too, although we sometimes end up talking about things that aren't strictly related to client work, as there is no-one there to keep us in check!

Kirsty points out some of the pros and cons of different methods. She refers to the power imbalance with her first internal line-manager supervisor, but goes on to say that this imbalance did not impact in a negative way on the supervisory relationship with her second line manager. She also mentions peer supervision and makes the point that discussions can sometimes go 'off track', as there is no named supervisor facilitating the sessions. Green (2010) reminds us that what is crucial to the effectiveness of supervision is the quality of the supervisory relationship, regardless of the particular method used. This can be said equally of the helper/client relationship. This is evidence again of the parallel process in practice.

Whilst the value of supervision to practitioner, organisation and client is clear, it is not the case that every helping professional receives supervision. As explained earlier, in some helping contexts supervision is mandatory (counselling, for instance) but the growth in the diversity of helping roles has not been matched by an acknowledgement of the importance of supervision, although there is some evidence that this is beginning to change (Hawkins and Shohet, 2006). Still, many who work in helping relationships do so unsupervised or with very little supervision. Where this is the case, helpers must ensure that they take any opportunities available to engage in continuing professional development activities.

Continuing professional development

The expression 'continuing professional development' (CPD) refers to any formal or informal training and development opportunities. The BACP requires counsellors, as they renew their accredited status each year, to list the CPD activities in which they have engaged, such is the importance of keeping practice up to date and reflective.

Activity: Continuing professional development – what is it and what are the benefits?

Write a list which details:

1. As full a range of what might constitute CPD activities as you can think of.
2. All the benefits CPD might bring to helpers and their clients.

CPD might take the form of formal training opportunities – either accredited training or short courses – but it can also include a much broader range of activities: for example, reading professional publications and journals, undertaking research into an area of interest, meeting with peers to discuss case work, and appraisals, reviews and so on. Where budgets in most helping professions are tight, opportunities for formal training can be difficult to negotiate. It is incumbent on every practitioner to seek out ways in which they can develop their knowledge and understanding further and review the skills that underpin their professional practice. In the testimony below, Chiara, a care support worker in a residential setting, reflects on her own CPD.

Case study: Chiara (care support worker) – CPD

I don't have access to supervision; the service was cut last year. I used to value the opportunity to talk about the clients who I am working closely with. A few of us got together and decided to set up our own peer support group. It's not the same as supervision, but it does give us a chance to talk about clients we are working with and to share ideas. I also keep my eye on our professional journal; training courses are advertised there and if I see something of interest and can make a strong case that it will benefit my practice, I take this to my line manager. My organisation has also set up a small library of professional texts to support our work. I can access these whenever I want to, and this is helpful. I have quarterly reviews and an annual appraisal with my line manager. These activities give me the opportunity to reflect on my practice and to think about what I'd like to develop further. My line manager suggested that I do a small-scale piece of research on support roles in residential settings. This interests me, but I need to think about how I can go about it. Long term, I'd like to study for a master's degree. I've mentioned this to my line manager and she is finding out whether I might be part-funded by my organisation. That would be fab!

Chiara offers a positive example of a helping professional who takes her own professional practice and development seriously. Although she no longer receives supervision, she has found ways to continue to reflect on and develop her practice. She is also aware of her own needs regarding her personal development. This is likely to help to keep her motivated and engaged in her work.

Getting the most from supervision and CPD

Even where organisations *are* able to provide quality supervision and a range of CPD opportunities, as supervision is an active and dynamic process, it is the responsibility of the helper to make the best use of these activities and use the time profitably.

Activity: Making best use of supervision

How might you prepare for each supervision session? What do you need to think about? What do you need to do?

On a very practical level, it is important that both supervisor and supervisee know where supervision is going to take place, the time of the session, and how long each session lasts. But there is more that supervisees need to prepare if they want to ensure that they get optimum results from the session. The list below helps to identify key elements that should be attended to.

- Before supervision, reflect on the presenting issues, challenges and successes of all the clients with whom you are working.
- Identify those that you would like to 'bring' to supervision (there may not be time to talk about every client, so select the ones where there are issues and challenges).
- Take time before supervision to think about how you would like to 'present' each case; this will avoid a hurried, muddled and garbled explanation.
- Be clear about what you need from your supervisor.
- Be open and honest about the work you have undertaken: attempting to cover 'mistakes' will not help issues to be addressed or practice to be developed.
- Take the opportunity to reflect in depth – share your thoughts and feelings, and use the time to analyse and process the work in detail.
- Draw on your knowledge of the theoretical underpinning to your work where appropriate.
- Use supervision to celebrate and learn from your successes.
- Be open to feedback: constructive criticism is helpful in developing best practice.
- Reflect and act upon what has been discussed in supervision – try new strategies and develop your use of skills in client practice.
- Be prepared to 'take risks' in supervision: using new and creative methods in supervision can serve to illuminate your client practice and offer ideas about different ways of working.

If these guidelines are adhered to, sessions are likely to be lively and productive. You will be engaged fully in the process and your skills of reflection will be heightened and developed. Furthermore, you should leave supervision feeling better able to re-engage with your client practice, whilst your own emotional equilibrium should feel restored to a greater or lesser extent. Dunnett *et al.* (2013: 47) suggest specific and general areas for reflection prior to supervision:

1. Specific areas for reflection:
   - What is going on for you with respect to a specific client, their story or behaviours?
   - Client material, behaviours or emotions generating raised anxiety or preoccupation in you, such as self-harm, suicidal thoughts, risky behaviour, extreme low mood, delusional thinking or uncontrollable anger.
   - What has worked well and what has not?
   - The context of your client's life and the location in which they are seen.
   - The counselling process: where is your client in their story?
   - Processes identified, such as 'stuckness' in either person, transference or countertransference.
   - Relationship quality and possible collusion.

2. General areas for reflection:
   - Too many or too few clients, since both situations have implications for practice and may require action.
   - Wonderings, specific questions, dilemmas, ethical issues, boundaries, professional relationships or organisational aspects.
   - Noticing what is brought regularly to supervision and what is normally left out.

Activity: Supervision in practice

Bearing the above points in mind, I would like you to go to Part II of the book now. Read through the real-life case studies provided by a range of helping practitioners. Select one, and think about how you would prepare to take this case to supervision. What would be the key issues you would like to focus on? What might you be feeling as a result of engaging with this client? How would you 'present' the narrative to your supervisor? What would you hope to get out of the supervision session?

This is a challenging activity and it serves to illustrate that the process of supervision does not simply happen within the hour-or-so session that you have with your supervisor. Much of the reflection will take place before, after and between the supervision sessions. The process of supervision sets out to support and develop heightened reflection and reflexivity on the part of the helper (see Chapter 6 for a full analysis of reflective and reflexive practice).

Likewise, helpers should ensure that they engage actively in CPD opportunities. For example, simply reading a journal article does not, in itself, constitute professional development. Reading, questioning, discussing, disagreeing and testing out are all activities that should take place alongside engaging with the text to optimise learning. Professional helpers who are able to enter fully into a dialogue with themselves, their colleagues, their supervisors, their teachers and others are likely to benefit from the rewards as they continue to develop as skilled and reflexive practitioners.

Summary

Although this is the final chapter in Part I of this book, it is an important one. It confirms that, as professional helpers, we have a responsibility to our clients – and we also have a responsibility to ourselves to continually seek ways to analyse, illuminate and develop our practice. Regular supervision is one activity that enables reflection and learning to take place; CPD is another. It is our responsibility to take advantage of, engage with and make good use of the opportunities that we have available to develop our knowledge, our understanding, our reflexivity and our skills. By so doing, we can ensure that we are continuing to give the best service possible to our clients and assist them to work towards positive change in their lives.

Further reading suggestions

Reid, H.L. and Westergaard, J. (2013) *Effective Supervision for Counsellors.* Exeter: Learning Matters – A helpful introductory text which outlines the purpose of supervision, the functions and the methods, and goes on to examine the development of the supervisory relationship.

Hawkins, P. and Shohet, R. (2006) *Supervision in the Helping Professions* (3rd edn). Maidenhead: Open University Press – A clearly written book on supervision that goes wider than looking at supervision in the counselling context, but acknowledges its place in the broader helping professions.

Dunnett, A., Jesper, C., O'Donnell, M. and Vallance, K. (2013) *Getting the Most from Supervision: A Guide for Counsellors and Psychotherapists.* Basingstoke: Palgrave Macmillan – A useful text written for supervisees.

PART II

ROLES IN THE HELPING PROFESSIONS

CASE STUDY 1

'ANNIE'

CONTRIBUTED BY A LEARNING SUPPORT ASSISTANT IN A MAINSTREAM SECONDARY SCHOOL

As a learning support assistant in a mainstream secondary school, I mentor young people with complex needs. Annie is a Year 8 pupil who struggles to control her anger and is prone to violent outbursts.

Having engaged with Annie for a year, we have built a very close working relationship. By listening closely to Annie and demonstrating empathy, respect and a non-judgemental approach, Annie has begun, over time, to trust me. She allows me 'into her world', to understand how she really feels behind the bravado. Annie is often lonely and frightened; her anger is her defence – she uses it to hurt others before they can hurt her.

My role as Annie's mentor is multifaceted, enabling her to develop coping strategies whilst occasionally advocating for her – whereby she trusts me to air her opinions appropriately. Together, by exploring Annie's thoughts and feelings, we have been working on anger management strategies and building her self-esteem. She is beginning to aspire to a positive future, whilst struggling to come to terms with her past.

Recently, Annie presented as angry and upset; but something about her body language was unusual. She seemed to be feeling anxious and uneasy too. Using the skill of active listening, and using gentle, open, probing questions, I began to 'hear' what Annie was *not* saying: she was talkative but there was little meaning to her words. I made the conscious decision to use the skill of immediacy to question Annie: 'Is there something on your mind that I could perhaps help you with? ... You seem to be talking lots, but not saying much?'

She replied: 'What would happen if I had brought something into school, Miss? Something that I shouldn't have done?'

Before I could answer, a noise outside the classroom startled Annie into an almost hysterical response. She ran into another room. As I followed her, she crawled under a table, backed up against the wall, and pulled a Stanley knife from her bag, which she began to run up and down her forearms.

I spoke calmly to Annie, ensuring that the tone of my voice was quiet and steady, listening intently and with empathy whilst she told me she wanted to end her life and had planned to do so in school that day. She spoke of how no-one would miss her and that it would make everything better if she went away. When she became quiet, I used the powerful skill of summarising to reflect back her own words. I went further – I described how I would miss her, and how her family might feel. I was probably the most open I have ever been with a pupil, and I believe that even through her fear and her pain, she responded to my congruent response. I explained why I wanted the knife, and empathised with how she felt – that I could see she was in pain, and reassured her that I was there for her. I explained that I could not take the pain away immediately, but that I would do everything I could to support her and to get her the help she was asking for.

I have no doubt that it was the effective application of counselling skills and the strength of our trusting relationship that ensured this situation ended positively.

The challenges of my job can mean that sometimes I feel out of my depth. It is difficult for me to witness the pain of a young person, knowing that I cannot make it cease. However, one of the greatest rewards is understanding that I can make a difference: engage with young people, take their lives seriously, treat them respectfully, and most of all – listen. Also, where appropriate, they can access the additional help and support they so desperately need and deserve.

Reflections

1. What would you have found challenging about working with Annie?
2. What skills and approaches are being demonstrated by Amy, the learning support assistant?
3. What ethical issues might Amy have to consider when working with Annie?
4. What are your thoughts about working in a school context with young people? What are the challenges and the rewards?

CASE STUDY 2

'MAGGIE'

CONTRIBUTED BY A LIFE-COACH IN PRIVATE PRACTICE

Maggie came to me as she was having major difficulties in her career and was facing imminent redundancy. Employed in a senior role, she was in a highly pressurised work environment, had problems with work colleagues, and had been through a period of great stress. Initially she asked for coaching around interview skills, as she wanted a new job but was still enmeshed in extricating herself from her last position.

Listening to Maggie describing the work problems that she had endured, and recounting both the pressure she was under and the unfair treatment she felt she had experienced from her employer, was an essential first task. There were tears in these early sessions, and the thought of confidently selling herself in the job market seemed impossible. Together we explored what she had been through, reflecting objectively on where her strengths lay, and began to plan for her recovery. Slowly, through careful listening and gentle challenging, Maggie began to regain her self-confidence and felt equipped to face the employment market again.

Helping someone to get over a difficult time can be very rewarding. Maggie is now confident and calm. Her sense of perspective enables her to deal with new, highly pressured responsibilities. She has progressed to a new role that is one step up from where she was when she first came to see me.

I enjoy work which is so 'in the present'. Planning how we will work together in sessions is a shared activity with clients, and there is little follow-up. I use all my helping skills 'in the moment', which is stimulating and satisfying. A key challenge of life-coaching is how to maintain a professional distance whilst still providing a close level of personal support over time. I cannot take over: clients have to find their own ways forward, albeit with my assistance.

In my role as Maggie's life-coach I represent a paid listener, supporter and mentor. This can mean using: counselling skills, as in our early meetings, to help explore problems; mentoring, to sit beside her and help her reflect on how her work, health and personal life are going; and coaching, to help her evaluate the best approach to forthcoming situations. I demonstrate empathy; I'm genuine and real in the relationship and I do not seek to judge; all whilst adopting a goal-focused model to encourage positive change. I use my experience of training and development for the mentoring role to guide and support, and I use management skills in coaching to facilitate planning and to motivate. These are used at different times, as appropriate. I often challenge and I use humour in my work with clients for a light touch.

Coaching frequently involves a prolonged relationship with a client. I saw Maggie every few months over a four-year period. She now comes to see me about once a year when she feels she needs some space to talk through what is happening in her life. She speaks often about the value of having a private space in which to reflect on the issues she faces and the support she feels she receives through our professional relationship.

Reflections

1. What would you have found challenging about working with Maggie?
2. What skills and approaches are being demonstrated by Becky, the life-coach?
3. What is your response to the statement that Becky is a 'paid listener'? What does 'support' mean in this context?
4. What are your thoughts about working as a life-coach? What are the challenges and the rewards?

CASE STUDY 3

'CALLER'

CONTRIBUTED BY A TELEPHONE HELPLINE COUNSELLOR

I have been a telephone counsellor for 18 months. What follows is an account of a call I had from a service user. The call lasted for two hours and I was very unsure if I could help this caller in the beginning. But armed with my strong belief in the person-centred approach and its core conditions of empathy, congruence and unconditional positive regard, I was able to accompany this caller through an extremely difficult journey.

I began with, 'Hello, can I help you?' This was followed by silence. Then in a very low, emotionless voice I was told that the caller did not think I could help. After about a minute, the caller attempted to talk but could only utter an occasional stuttering word, then more silence. I assured the caller that everything they told me was confidential and was only shared within the service. I then asked the caller, 'Can you tell me why you called today?' I hoped this would help the caller to focus, as I felt they may be feeling overwhelmed and may not know where to start. I also understood how difficult it must be to tell a complete stranger your innermost thoughts and feelings.

The caller continued to talk, very quietly with the same flat tone, which began to get louder, faster and angrier. I had to check myself here as I have trouble dealing with anger and did not want to react in a way that would make the caller feel challenged or confronted. Although protocol states that counsellors do not have to accept hostile or abusive behaviour and can end calls if they feel threatened, I felt this caller's anger was aimed at their situation and not at me. I continued listening, offering only para-verbal responses to encourage the caller to tell their story. It was like the 'flood gates' had been opened. This caller went from barely talking, to pouring out their soul to me. I felt privileged that they could trust me enough to take me on their journey with them.

At first the caller was angry at everything: doctors, family, friends and so on. The caller jumped from one thing to another and did not make a lot of sense at times. The pace was very fast at first, but the more the caller was able to talk, the slower the pace became. The caller's voice calmed and they started to speak more rationally. I felt this was the point where I could start to challenge some of the caller's thoughts and feelings. I understood the caller was angry but I felt the anger was a 'cover-up' for a deeper emotion the caller was struggling with. I started to ask the caller questions like, 'Could you explain that further?' when I felt they were stopping short of a deeper meaning, and, 'What makes you think/feel that?' when the caller's reason seemed to be a little irrational, and also summarising and paraphrasing to gain clarification.

The caller's thinking became clearer as the process went on. Yes, they felt angry, but this was fuelled by the frustration that no-one could help them change their situation – not their doctor, family or friends. Also the caller was frustrated that they felt unable to talk to people about this. Finally the caller was able to reveal their deepest feeling: they were scared. The caller explained that they had a decision to make – if they chose one path it may improve their life, or it may not and things could get worse, but if they chose to do nothing it was certain to get worse.

I may not have been able to 'fix' things, but I was able to help the caller accept their situation and consider their options more rationally. Towards the end of the call the caller's voice was quiet and calm. I continued to listen and allowed small silences to enable time for reflection. When the caller decided it was time to go, they thanked me for listening and said goodbye.

Reflections

1. What would you have found challenging about working with this caller?
2. What skills and approaches are being demonstrated by Deb, the telephone helpline counsellor?
3. What might some of the ethical issues be in this field of practice?
4. What are your thoughts about working on a telephone counselling hotline? What are the challenges and the rewards?

CASE STUDY 4

'DIANE'

CONTRIBUTED BY AN NHS COMMUNITY DRUGS AND ALCOHOL WORKER

I am employed as a drug worker in an NHS community drug and alcohol service. The team is multidisciplinary, consisting of psychiatrists, community psychiatric nurses, family therapists, psychologists and drug workers. Our clients are considered 'complex' in that they have dual diagnoses of mental health and substance-use disorders, often coupled with additional social problems such as poverty and homelessness.

I work with a young woman who has a diagnosis of personality disorder, opiate and crack cocaine dependency. When I first met Diane, 18 months ago, she seemed wary. She had worked with a previous keyworker for two years and formed a close attachment to him. I took time to get to know her, ensuring that I demonstrated empathy, was genuine and showed her unconditional positive regard. I asked her about her relationship with her previous keyworker in order that I could maintain interventions that she had found helpful. I also arranged to meet her together with her previous keyworker, so that she could begin to feel safe with me. This was a very important part of the engagement process, as Diane had suffered many losses in her life and I knew that 'letting go' of attachments was difficult for her.

I noticed that Diane had burns on her arms, caused by holding her arms over a cooker. This happens when she is distressed, in response to a voice in her head telling her to hurt herself. She names the voice 'Annie'. I spent time with her, showing empathy by actively listening to her story and working with her to identify triggers which seem to increase stress and are likely to lead her to thinking about harming herself. We also discussed the role of crack cocaine in increasing her stress levels. Together, we explored her thoughts, feelings and behaviour to increase her awareness of the interaction between cocaine use and mental health, particularly its negative impact on mood and impulse control.

I organised a medical review with our psychiatrist, who increased the dose of Diane's antipsychotic medication, and I encouraged her to seek assistance from our psychologist, always ensuring that Diane was supported in taking responsibility for her decision making and actions.

During our keywork sessions I enabled Diane to increase her resilience and coping skills by working collaboratively on problem-solving techniques. One example was when her pharmacist accused her of stealing. She felt that she had made a genuine mistake and was now feeling sad about not being trusted. Also, she felt uncomfortable every time she walked into the chemist to collect her medication. By using open and hypothetical questioning techniques and sharing information, we reflected together on how she might deal with the situation, and we brainstormed possible strategies. Diane evaluated the pros and cons of each strategy. She chose the option of asking the pharmacist if she could talk to him, as she had known him for some time and felt that he might be receptive to hearing about her perspective on the alleged theft incident.

She was anxious about this strategy so we rehearsed what she might say. I was really pleased to hear that she did speak to the pharmacist, and they repaired their relationship. This gave her a real sense of achievement as she had talked about and faced her fears. This is something that she is able to reflect upon as she faces other challenges.

Diane benefited from receiving co-ordinated interventions from multidisciplinary teamwork and is now clean from all illicit drug use and is no longer self-harming.

Reflections

1. What would you have found challenging about working with Diane?
2. What skills and approaches are being demonstrated by Georgia, the NHS community drugs and alcohol worker?
3. Georgia talks about the difficulties Diane had in accepting her as a new helper. Why might this be?
4. What are your thoughts about working in the field of addictions? What are the challenges and the rewards?

CASE STUDY 5

'KANE'

CONTRIBUTED BY A TEACHER IN A CHILDREN'S HOSPITAL

I have been a qualified teacher for five years. Until recently I worked in a mainstream comprehensive; I now work in a children's hospital. This means I teach children who are admitted to hospital as in-patients. Generally, this is done one to one at their bedside, as most children who are in hospital for this length of time are not able to leave their rooms. Instead of the pupil entering the teacher's domain (the classroom) the teacher enters the pupil's domain (their bedroom for the duration of their stay).

I had not been in the job long when I met Kane. He was a patient who would be in and out for a few months before being admitted for a prolonged stay. He was 12 years old and not long into his secondary education. When we first met he was, very clearly, uninterested by the prospect of school. He did not want it and I doubt he saw the point of it, in his situation.

One of the basic foundations of teaching is to help a child go from point A to point B, where point B shows greater understanding than point A. As a teacher you need to know what point A looks like before you can know how to get to point B. To do this, you ask questions. Sadly, Kane was reluctant to make me aware of where his point A was, and greeted every one of my questions with the answer 'I don't know'.

I had to ask *myself* a question at this point: 'Who is this person I am trying to educate?' It is not a question teachers generally have time to ask of every pupil they work with in mainstream education, and it is not a question I always have to ask myself in this job. Some pupils accept without question your presence in their personal space and the work you bring them. But not Kane.

Through using gentle and open questions with him, I began to discover where his interests lay. I listened actively to his responses – what he was saying verbally, and what his body language was telling me – and I began to build a bond with him and understand what he cared about and what he did not care about. At this point the focus was on Kane and building that relationship of trust. I needed to be empathic to Kane's situation and show him that I understood how he was feeling and was interested in him as a fellow human being. I then tailored the work we did to the areas he cared about, so that he would be more likely to continue to engage with both me and his education during his time in hospital. I began to really think about the way I need to make children feel about my presence in their world at a time when the last thing they would be thinking about is their education. This means I have adapted my skill-set and focused more on being passionate and fully engaged with the child in front of me as well as the subject I am teaching.

Over the course of the next six months, through his various stays in hospital, we built a very good working relationship and Kane engaged with school, made progress in his understanding, and developed a new love for a subject he had never before cared about. In the thank-you card he gave me on his discharge, he said 'You made school interesting for me.' When we first met each other, I don't think either of us thought this possible.

Reflections

1. What would you have found challenging about working with Kane?
2. What skills and approaches are being demonstrated by James, the hospital teacher?
3. James's role is to educate, but Kane is at first reluctant to engage and James becomes a 'helper' in his efforts to establish a relationship. How important is the therapeutic relationship in this case?
4. What are your thoughts about working in education within a health setting? What are the challenges and the rewards?

CASE STUDY 6

'LETCHME'

CONTRIBUTED BY A REGISTERED MANAGER OF A CHILDREN'S HOME

In my role as a registered manager of a children's home, I support young people with emotional and behavioural difficulties and associated complex needs. My work with Letchme has been both demanding and rewarding. Letchme was 13 years of age when she came to the children's home. She had disclosed serious sexual abuse.

Letchme's Sikh family lived as a community. Her parents' marriage was arranged by the family. Letchme's mother had suffered physical abuse from the day she moved in with the family. She recalls giving birth to her daughter in hospital and being pleased to be told that Letchme had slight jaundice and would need to stay in the hospital for a few days. Her mother was grateful for the time they would have together. The family were disappointed that Letchme was not a boy. Her mother would be punished emotionally and physically for failing to produce a son. Her mother was forbidden to nurse Letchme: her role was to keep the home clean; the elder women in the family took care of Letchme. Her mother was beaten and broken – she left the family in the belief that Letchme would be cared for by her female relatives, until she planned to return and take Letchme to live with her.

The family brought Letchme up, leading her to believe that her mother was dead. Letchme suffered sexual abuse from her male relations, and for much of her life believed this was normal behaviour; she knew no different.

My work with Letchme includes supporting her through the trauma of court proceedings, keeping her safe from her paternal family, and assisting her to build a relationship with her mother, with whom she is now in contact. Letchme has been diagnosed with post-traumatic stress disorder and attachment disorder. She is angry with her mother for leaving her to be abused and will not accept that her mother did what she thought was best for them both at the time. I spend many hours listening to Letchme – not only her spoken word but also the things expressed in her actions. She will sit close to staff when her mother visits, choosing the furthest point from her mother to be seated. Letchme will reflect with me after these visits. We have built a therapeutic alliance; she trusts me and we agree to be open and honest with one another. I have been able to use role play to re-enact Letchme's behaviour during her mother's visits to assist her reflection. I often paraphrase the challenging things Letchme says to her mother: 'Drop dead. Don't come back. I hate you.' I empathise with how she is feeling. I suggest that I will not arrange further visits as this causes her such pain. Letchme will cry and tell me she didn't mean what she said. We begin to work together to identify strategies which may help her overcome her past and move on to a positive future.

I have a long road ahead with Letchme. She has refused to engage with counselling other than our sessions. I worry that I am not a qualified counsellor, but a helper who listens. But I use my own supervision to understand that by listening, supporting and encouraging Letchme, I am making a small difference to a very important life. Letchme's feelings of low self-worth are *her* feelings; to me she is an endearing and spirited young person with a bright future to embrace.

Reflections

1. What would you have found challenging about working with Letchme?
2. What skills and approaches were being demonstrated by Kim, the manager of the children's home?
3. What might be the possible impact of cultural issues in this case?
4. What are your thoughts about working in the field of social care? What are the challenges and the rewards?

CASE STUDY 7

'AMY'

CONTRIBUTED BY A COUNSELLOR AND COACH THERAPIST IN PRIVATE PRACTICE

Amy is a young white woman in her early thirties with a highly successful, but often very stressful, job in the financial sector. Though actively ambitious and highly sought-after for new positions both in and out of the company, Amy has experienced some debilitating times of overwhelming anxiety in recent months. She found out about me as a coach through my website.

I qualified as an executive and personal coach six years ago and trained as a therapist over 20 years ago. People approach me for coaching and understand that I may also at times offer some therapeutic work in the service of going forward with their coaching goals. I use an integrative process as a framework to support my practice. My approach appealed to Amy, as she wanted help both with current challenges at work and to talk about issues from her family of origin.

I explain to clients, in a pre-coaching call, that an integrative approach enables me to listen actively and deeply to support them to rebalance (in terms of emotions, thoughts and behaviours), generate possibilities and take action to make sustainable changes. A key challenge here is to assess whether this approach is appropriate, and to negotiate the right balance between interventions normally associated with coaching and those associated with therapy. Some clients have had counselling in the past, which many have found useful, and they are now seeking something to help them move forward more explicitly. However, some clients would not be attracted to therapy but do recognise a need for some emotional and psychological support and exploration.

In the first session, I listened attentively as Amy shared her reflections and thoughts and we acknowledged her existing strengths and achievements, highlighting transferable skills to draw on in the rest of the work. I used solution-focused questions to establish what was already going well, where Amy would like to be in a specific area, and what the signs of progress towards that end would be.

There were two key areas of focus. One was some dissonance with how she was perceived at work as a team member and a leader (intimidating, dynamic, self-contained), with her internal perception of feeling at times very anxious and vulnerable. This anxiety particularly gripped her whenever she had to make formal presentations. She drove herself very hard and worked long hours.

The other was in relation to issues in her family of origin. Amy had suffered from extensive bullying at school but felt her needs at that time were not as important as her brother, who struggled with issues leading to quite serious self-harm. I noted after the session that I had 'challenged the view that Amy's needs were relatively less important, and [that] Amy cried and looked very intensely into my eyes'.

Following this session we contracted to work more frequently and for shorter sessions for a few weeks (counselling approach) whilst we were dealing with powerful, previously unexpressed emotions originating in stresses from the past relating to issues of mental health in her birth family. We would re-contract later for longer sessions, further apart, with more of a coaching approach.

Through using exercises and mindfulness Amy learned to cope with making presentations at work without having to use beta-blockers. She recognised that she needed time alone to prepare for work presentations and to recharge. She also made time for exercise and doing enjoyable things with her partner. She had been able to talk about her feelings with her family, and felt both less responsible for making them feel better, and more able to accept herself and them, which meant that the relationships were more relaxed.

At the end of our work together Amy was sleeping well and listening to her own needs. She was looking forward to the future, and having secured and done well in her 'dream job', she was beginning to think about starting a family.

Reflections

1. What would you have found challenging about working with Amy?
2. What skills and approaches were being demonstrated by Carolyn, the coach therapist?
3. What are your thoughts about the way in which Carolyn uses both counselling and coaching approaches in her work?
4. What are your thoughts about working in this therapeutic field of practice? What are the challenges and the rewards?

CASE STUDY 8

'JOE'

CONTRIBUTED BY A TRAINEE PROBATION OFFICER

I am currently working for the National Probation Service (NPS) as a trainee probation officer. The majority of my role is offender management.

As an offender manager (OM) in the NPS, my role is to work with high-risk offenders who are serving court-ordered community and custodial sentences, including the licence period completed after release from prison. The purpose of my role is to assess criminogenic needs, devise a plan to support the offender through their sentence, enforce any breaches of their requirements, and continually assess and manage the risks they pose.

My case study focuses on Joe, a young man I have been supporting since his release from custody. He is classed as high-risk, owing to his significant amount of previous convictions and the range of needs identified when assessed. In previous reports Joe was considered a risk to staff because of his abusive behaviour towards police and previous threats towards a probation officer. Before our initial appointment I felt nervous about meeting Joe, but I made a conscious effort to remain open and to empathise, as I wanted build a positive relationship with him.

Joe arrived two hours late and heavily intoxicated for his initial appointment. I was required to issue a warning about this and we agreed the appointment should be moved to the following morning. Joe accepted this and arrived the next day on time and in a coherent state. When warning Joe about his intoxication, I explicitly explained the expectations of probation. He recognised that attending appointments when substance-affected would be unhelpful. We agreed that our appointments would be early mornings and if possible on regular days each week. I explained that if Joe continued to attend his appointments, in four weeks the warning could be removed if he engaged positively. This felt like a positive start to the relationship.

Whilst working to build an open and trusting relationship with Joe, he spoke freely of his previous negative experiences with probation, and how he had been told in court he was 'unworkable' and therefore felt excluded by the service. I acknowledged his feelings of frustration and reassured him that I would like to make this a positive experience. I emphasised that I did not accept him being labelled as 'unworkable'.

Over the next three weeks Joe opened up about his life history: how he had been abused by previous foster carers, spent time in a number of care homes all around the country, had experienced a disrupted education, and had begun to drink alcohol and use drugs at 14 to help him cope emotionally. He was initially 'closed' and guarded about his past, but by my attending to Joe – using open questions and appropriate body language, and expressing genuine interest – he began to feel safe to discuss these difficult times.

I also arranged a professionals meeting which included his hostel keyworker, police and substance misuse worker. This meeting was really useful, as we were able to formulate a plan as how to best support Joe. The main focus was to help him decrease his drug and alcohol use safely, and alongside this introduce emotional coping strategies, whilst referring him for formal counselling.

In the following appointment I planned to introduce this plan to Joe, and, as change has to be driven and directed by the client, seek his agreement. However, Joe failed to attend the appointment. Three days later he was convicted of two further offences of criminal damage. This meant he was returned to custody for a period of 14 days. The decision to return to custody was difficult as I was concerned about its potential impact on our relationship. But the pressures from management meant that I had limited discretion in the decision-making process.

Following his release, Joe has continued to engage with me. His drug and alcohol use continue to be problematic, but plans are being made for residential rehabilitation at his request. I hope that with a continued multi-agency approach this goal can be achieved and Joe can complete his licence period successfully.

Reflections

1. What would you have found challenging about working with Joe?
2. What skills and approaches are being demonstrated by Sally, the probation officer?
3. What ethical issues does Sally raise when her work with Joe is disrupted?
4. What are your thoughts about working in the criminal justice field of practice? What are the challenges and the rewards?

CASE STUDY 9

'MEGAN'

CONTRIBUTED BY A CARE MANAGER ASSISTANT

I am employed as a care manager assistant in a multidisciplinary health and social care team, working with adults with learning disabilities. Our team consists of care managers, community nurses, occupational therapists, speech and language therapists, psychologists and counsellors. The team provides a person-centred approach to support planning, adopting a holistic approach to meeting clients' needs and aspirations.

I was asked to see a young woman, 'Megan', who had visited a local drop-in centre for people with learning disabilities. She appears distant and isolated from the group and presents as very low.

Megan seems reluctant to talk to me. In our initial interventions she looks away and does not engage in conversation. Even though she does not want to speak, we sit together, and it becomes clear that she is comfortable, listening and attending. After several weeks, most of our time in silence, she begins to tell her 'story'.

Megan explains that she lives at home with her father, stepmother and young brother. Megan says that she hates her stepmother, who calls her names and tells her she is useless and stupid. She tells me that she used to enjoy going to college; however, on the day of her exams, her stepmother gave her some 'special chocolate' that made her ill and she left with no qualifications. Megan says that she does all the cooking and cleaning in the house and she is not allowed to go out unless her stepmother gives her permission. She attends the local drop-in centre in secret when fetching the shopping. She is told to babysit her young brother and take him to school every day. She has no money or bank account, as her father is in control of all her benefits. In the evenings her stepmother tells her to stay in her room. Her father explains that he is protecting her by controlling her life, because she was sexually abused as a child and she might be vulnerable. Megan is very unhappy and her self-esteem and confidence are low.

As the listener, Megan's story is very difficult to hear. I experience a natural feeling of wanting to instantly 'fix' the situation for her. However, Megan makes it clear that she does not want anyone to 'interfere' in her life or tell her what to do, and that if I do, she will not come back. Over several weeks of actively listening and helping Megan to reflect, I begin to notice changes in her behaviour. Our relationship develops. Megan appears to be able to 'trust' the space we have created and feels comfortable to explore her inner thoughts. Asking open questions enables Megan to begin to evaluate her life and challenge the perceptions and motives of others. She needs to find strength from within, to enable her to move forward. Her life has been controlled and now she is enabled to make her own choices and decisions; Megan starts to reflect and grow emotionally. Using hypothetical questions and the skill of challenge, Megan explores how her life might look in the future. She begins to consider her options and make decisions and plans.

After several months, Megan makes the decision to leave the family home and start a new life living independently. I, together with colleagues, support Megan with the practical aspects of moving on, but she chooses to tell her family of her decision by herself. She has now returned to college to finish her exams.

Megan is empowered to take control of her life and find solutions to her problems. She wants to be accepted for who she is, as a unique and valued human being, not just someone with a 'learning disability'. For those with diverse and complex needs, like Megan, the impact and significance of active listening is often overlooked. Megan's voice was 'heard' for the first time. The power of demonstrating empathy, congruence and unconditional positive regard both enabled Megan to feel valued as an individual and empowered her to make changes in her life.

Reflections

1. What would you have found challenging about working with Megan?
2. What skills and approaches are being demonstrated by Sarah, the care manager assistant?
3. What are the ethical challenges of working in a multidisciplinary health and social care team, as Sarah does with Megan?
4. What are your thoughts about working in a multidisciplinary health and social care team? What are the challenges and the rewards?

CASE STUDY 10

'KANTA'

CONTRIBUTED BY A SURGICAL NURSE SPECIALIST

I work as a surgical nurse specialist for the NHS. Part of my role involves visiting patients who are recovering from surgery and require further treatment and support in their own homes. Generally I have two or three visits, before the patient is deemed well enough to manage any on-going treatment and recovery without my support. This means that I have to build relationships with patients very quickly. This can be challenging, as I am often supporting people who have undergone treatment that has resulted in a physical disfigurement, in particular, women who have had surgery for breast cancer.

Kanta was one such woman. I visited Kanta in her home on three occasions in total. Kanta underwent a mastectomy and had her left breast removed. On my first visit, Kanta had still not been able to look in the mirror at her changed body. She was in distress, in tears and feeling both desperate and negative and unable to accept the reality of her changed body.

On my fist visit, I did very little apart from listen to Kanta and sit alongside her pain. I tried to avoid saying things like, 'It'll be fine' and, 'Don't worry, reconstruction is an option' because I knew she needed time to grieve her physical loss and to begin to accept her altered appearance. I did reassure Kanta that what she was feeling was perfectly normal, and that many women experience feelings akin to bereavement when they have had this kind of surgery. But I realised that it didn't matter what I said at that stage: Kanta was too immersed in her grief, and nothing I could do or say would take that pain away. When I left, Kanta grabbed my hand and thanked me for just being with her and understanding her pain. She explained that everyone else is trying to 'jolly me along' and that 'I'm trying to be strong for everyone else, you know, family and friends.'

On my next visit, Kanta asked if I would be with her when she looked at the wound for the first time. I helped Kanta to reflect on what it might feel like for her to see her altered image and I made sure that I did not hurry the process. I also reassured her that different people have very different responses and that there's not a 'right way' to feel. Once Kanta felt ready, we went to her bedroom and, very slowly, I helped Kanta to undress the wound. She asked me to hold her hand as she looked in the mirror for the first time, which I did. I wouldn't naturally make this kind of gesture, because not all patients want or need this kind of physical intimacy, but for Kanta it was important and I was happy to respond to her need.

To begin with, Kanta stood quietly and just stared at herself. After a period of silence, I gently asked Kanta how it felt for her to see her body. She didn't reply straight away and I remained quiet to give her time to absorb and reflect on her physical image and her initial emotional response. I was mindful of Kanta's body language and facial expressions throughout this process and I tried to really listen to her unspoken communication. After some minutes, Kanta turned to me and said, 'It's OK, isn't it? It's OK.'

On my final visit, some weeks later, I assisted Kanta to fit a soft temporary prosthesis in her bra. She was in a much more positive place and thanked me for my care and support.

Reflections

1. What would you have found challenging about working with Kanta?
2. What skills and approaches are being demonstrated by Cindy, the surgical nurse specialist?
3. Cindy talks about 'sitting alongside her client's pain'. How might it feel to do this?
4. What are your thoughts about working in the health professions? What are the challenges and the rewards?

REFERENCES

Alred, G., Garvey, B. and Smith, R. (1998) *Mentoring Pocketbook*. Alresford: Management Pocketbooks.

Arulmani, G. (2009) 'A matter of culture', *Career Guidance Today* (Institute of Career Guidance), 17 (1) March: 1–12.

BACP (British Association for Counselling and Psychotherapy) (2010) *Ethical Framework for Good Practice in Counselling and Psychotherapy*. Rugby: BACP.

BACP (British Association of Counselling and Psychotherapy) (2015) *Ethical Framework for Good Practice in Counselling and Psychotherapy*. Lutterworth: BACP.

Banks, S. (2001) *Ethics and Values in Social Work* (2nd edn). Basingstoke: Palgrave.

Banks, S. (2012) *Ethics and Values in Social Work* (4th edn). Basingstoke: Palgrave.

Bassot, B. (2013) *The Reflective Journal*. Basingstoke: Palgrave Macmillan.

Beauchamp, T.L. and Childress, J.F. (2008) *Principles of Biomedical Ethics* (6th edn). New York: Oxford University Press.

Bond, T. (2015) *Standards and Ethics for Counselling in Action* (4th edn). London: Sage.

Borton, T. (1970) *Reach, Touch and Teach*. London: Hutchinson.

Cameron, H. (2008) *The Counselling Interview: A Guide for the Helping Professions*. Basingstoke: Palgrave Macmillan.

Claringbull, N. (2010) *What is Counselling and Psychotherapy?* Exeter: Learning Matters.

Clutterbuck, D. and Megginson, D. (1999) *Mentoring Executives and Directors*. Oxford: Butterworh Heinemann.

Cooper, M. and Wheeler, M.M. (2010) 'Building successful mentoring relationships', *The Canadian Nurse*, 106 (7): 34–5.

Cox, E., Bachkirova, T. and Clutterbuck, D. (2014) *The Complete Handbook of Coaching* (2nd edn). London: Sage.

Culley, S. and Bond, T. (2004) *Integrative Counselling Skills in Action* (2nd edn). London: Sage.

Culley, S. and Bond, T. (2011) *Integrative Counselling Skills in Action* (3rd edn). London: Sage.

D'Andrea, M. and Daniels, J. (1991) 'Evaluating the impact of multicultural counselling training', *Journal of Counseling and Development*, 70(1): 143–50.

David, S., Clutterbuck, D. and Megginson, D. (2013) *Beyond Goals: Effective Strategies for Coaching and Mentoring*. Aldershot: Gower.

de Haan, E. (2008) *Relational Coaching: Journeys Towards Mastering One-to-One Learning*. New York: John Wiley and Sons.

Downey, M. (2003) *Effective Coaching: Lessons from the Coach's Coach*. Knutsford: Texere Publishing.

Driscoll, J. (ed.) (2007) *Practising Clinical Supervision: A Reflective Approach for Healthcare Professionals*. Edinburgh: Baillière Tindall, Elsevier.

Dunnett, A., Jesper, C., O'Donnell, M. and Vallance, K. (2013) *Getting the Most from Supervision: A Guide for Counsellors and Psychotherapists*. Basingstoke: Palgrave Macmillan.

Egan, G. (2007) *The Skilled Helper: A Problem-Management and Opportunity-Development Approach to Helping* (8th edn). Pacific Grove, CA: Brooks/Cole.

Eysenck, H.J. (1970) 'A mish-mash of theories', *International Journal of Psychiatry*, 9: 140–6.

Feltham, C. (2012) 'What are counselling and psychotherapy?', in C. Feltham and I. Horton (eds), *The SAGE Handbook of Counselling and Psychotherapy*. London: Sage. p. 13.

Fook, J. and Askeland, G. (2006) 'The "critical" in critical reflection', in S. White, J. Fook and F. Gardner (eds), *Critical Reflection in Health and Social Care*. Maidenhead: Open University Press. pp. 40–53.

Garvey, B., Stokes, P. and Megginson, D. (2014) *Coaching and Mentoring: Theory and Practice* (2nd edn). London: Sage.

Geldard, K. and Geldard, D. (2005) *Practical Counselling Skills: An integrative Approach*. Basingstoke: Palgrave Macmillan.

George, H. (2015) 'You don't talk your business to people', *Therapy Today*, 26 (9): 12–16.

Ghaye, T. (2011) *Teaching and Learning through Reflective Practice: A Practical Guide for Positive Action*. Abingdon: Routledge.

Gibbs, G. (1998) *Learning by Doing: A Guide to Teaching and Learning Methods*. Oxford: Further Education Unit, Oxford Polytechnic.

Grant, A.M. (2006) 'Solution-focused coaching', in J. Passmore (ed.), *Excellence in Coaching*. London: Kogan Page. pp. 73–90.

Green, J. (2010) *Creating the Therapeutic Relationship in Counselling and Psychotherapy*. Exeter: Learning Matters.

Hanley, T. (2012) 'Understanding the on-line therapeutic alliance through the eyes of adolescent service users', *Counselling and Psychotherapy Research*, 12 (1): 35–43.

Hawkins, P. and Shohet, R. (2000) *Supervision in the Helping Professions* (2nd edn). Maidenhead: Open University Press.

Hawkins, P. and Shohet, R. (2006) *Supervision in the Helping Professions* (3rd edn). Maidenhead: Open University Press.

Haynes, F. (1998) *The Ethical School*. London: Routledge.

Hollanders, H. (2014) 'Integrative therapy', in W. Dryden and A. Reeves (eds), *The Handbook of Individual Therapy* (6th edn). London: Sage. pp. 519–45.

Inskipp, F. and Proctor, B. (1993) *The Art, Craft and Tasks of Counselling Supervision, Part 1: Making the Most of Supervision*. Twickenham: Cascade Publications.

Jenkins, P. (2007) 'Gerard Egan's Skilled Helper Model', in S. Palmer and R. Wolfe (eds), *Integrative and Eclectic Psychotherapy*. London: Sage. pp. 163–80.

Johns, C. (1994) 'Nuances of reflection', *Journal of Clinical Nursing*, 3: 71–5.

Johns, C. (2004) *Becoming a Reflective Practitioner* (2nd edn). Oxford: Blackwell Publishing.

Johns, C. (2013) *Becoming a Reflective Practitioner* (4th edn). Oxford: Wiley.

Kadushin, A. (1992) *Supervision in Social Work* (3rd edn). New York: Columbia University Press.

Kolb, D. (1984) *Experiential Learning: Experience as the Source of Learning and Development*. Upper Saddle River, NJ: Prentice Hall.

Lynass, R., Pykhtina, O. and Cooper, M. (2012) 'A thematic analysis of young people's experience of counselling in five secondary schools in the UK', *Counselling and Psychotherapy Research*, 12 (1): 53–62.

McLeod, J. (1998) *An Introduction to Counselling* (2nd edn). Buckingham: Open University Press.

McLeod, J. (2004) *An Introduction to Counselling* (3rd edn). Buckingham: Open University Press.

Mearns, D. and Cooper, M. (2005) *Working at Relational Depth in Counselling and Psychotherapy*. London: Sage.

Mearns, D. and Thorne, B. (2013) *Person-Centred Counselling in Action* (4th edn). London: Sage.

Mezirow, J. (1978) *Education for Perspective Transformation: Women's Reentry Programs in Community Colleges*. New York: Centre for Adult Education, Columbia University.

Mezirow, J. (1981) 'A critical theory of adult learning and education', *Adult Education*, 32 (1): 13–24.

Monk, G., Winslade, J. and Sinclair, S. (2008) *New Horizons in Multicultural Counselling*. Thousand Oaks, CA: Sage.

Murphy, K. and Gilbert, M. (2000) 'A systematic integrative relational model for counselling and psychotherapy', in S. Palmer and R. Wolfe (eds), *Integrative and Eclectic Psychotherapy*. London: Sage. pp. 93–109.

Nelson-Jones, R. (2012) *Basic Counselling Skills: A Helper's Manual*. London: Sage.

Osborne, T. (1998) 'Constructionism, authority and the ethical life', in I. Velody and R. Williams (eds), *The Politics of Constructionism*. London: Sage.

Pask, R. and Joy, B. (2007) *Mentoring-Coaching: A Guide for Education Professionals*. Maidenhead: Open University Press.

Prever, M. (2010) *Counselling and Supporting Children and Young People: A Person-Centred Approach*. London: Sage.

Reid, H.L. (2015) *Introduction to Career Counselling and Coaching*. London: Sage.

Reid, H.L. and Fielding, A.J. (2007) *Providing Support to Young People: A Guide to Interviewing in Helping Relationships*. London: Routledge.

Reid, H.L. and Westergaard, J. (2011) *Effective Counselling with Young People*. Exeter: Learning Matters.

Reid, H.L. and Westergaard, J. (2013) *Effective Supervision for Counsellors*. Exeter: Learning Matters.

Rogers, C. (1951) *Client-Centred Therapy: Its Current Practice, Implications and Theory*. Boston, MA: Houghton Mifflin.

Rogers, C. (1961) *On Becoming a Person*. Boston, MA: Houghton Mifflin.

Rogers, C. and Stevens, B. (1967) *Person to Person: The Problem of Being Human.* Lafayette, CA: Real People Press.

Schön, D.A. (1983) *The Reflective Practitioner.* Aldershot: Ashgate.

Stadler, H.A. (1986) *Confidentiality: The Professional's Dilemma – Participant's Manual.* Alexandria, VA: American Association for Counseling and Development.

Sue, D.W., Ivey, A.E. and Pederson, P.B. (1996) *A Theory of Multicultural Counseling and Therapy.* Pacific Grove, CA: Brooks/Cole.

Szasz, T.S. (1974) *The Ethics of Psychoanalysis: The Theory and Method of Autonomous Psychotherapy.* London: Routledge and Kegan Paul.

Talbot, N., Pahlevan, B. and Boyles, J. (2015) 'We cannot talk if we do not feel free,' *Therapy Today,* 26 (9): 12–17.

Thompson, A. (1990) *A Guide to Ethical Practice in Psychotherapy.* New York: John Wiley and Sons.

Thompson, N. (2011) *Promoting Equality: Working with Diversity and Difference* (3rd edn). Basingstoke: Palgrave Macmillan.

Thompson, S. and Thompson, P (2008) *The Critically Reflective Practitioner.* Basingstoke: Palgrave Macmillan.

United Kingdom Council for Psychotherapy (2009) *UKCP Ethical Principles and Code of Ethical Conduct.* London: UKCP.

van Nieuwerburgh, C. (2014) *An Introduction to Counselling Skills: A Practical Guide.* London: Sage.

Whitmore, J. (1992) *Coaching for Performance: A Practical Guide to Growing Your Own Skills.* London: Nicholas Brealey.

Whitmore, J. (2009) *Coaching for Performance: GROWing Human Potential and Purpose* (4th edn). London: Nicholas Brealey.

Wilkins, P. (2001) 'Unconditional positive regard reconsidered', in J.D. Bozarth and P. Wilkins (eds), *Rogers' Therapeutic Conditions: Evolution, Theory and Practice – Unconditional Positive Regard.* Ross-on-Wye: PCCS Books. (First published in 2000 in *British Journal of Guidance and Counselling,* 28 (1): 23–36.)

Worsley, R. (2007) *The Integrative Counselling Primer: A Concise, Accessible and Comprehensive Introduction to Integrative Counselling with a Person-Centred Foundation.* Ross-on-Wye: PCCS Books.

Zachary, L.J. (2000) *The Mentor's Guide.* San Francisco, CA: Jossey-Bass.

INDEX